Saturdays with Father Schall

On Fatherhood, Intellectual Life, and Friendship

Fr. Stefanus Hendrianto, S.J., PhD

En Route Books and Media, LLC
Saint Louis, MO

⊕ENROUTE
Make the time

En Route Books and Media, LLC

5705 Rhodes Avenue

St. Louis, MO 63109

Contact us at contactus@enroutebooksandmedia.com

Cover Credit: Sebastian Mahfood using an image of Sacred Heart Statue at the Sacred Heart Jesuit Center in Los Gatos

Copyright 2024 Stefanus Hendrianto

ISBN-13: 979-8-88870-269-7

Library of Congress Control Number: 2024950650

Table of Contents

Preface

This book was born out of an essay that I wrote on the occasion of the 90th birthday of Fr. Schall, titled *Saturdays with Fr. Schall: A Young Jesuit on the Older Jesuit's 90th Birthday*.[1] In December 2018, Fr. Schall seemed to be in his final days on earth after having surgery to deal with the agonizing problem of a twisted colon. When I was visiting him at the Jesuit infirmary of Los Gatos, California, I began to think about finding the best way to say goodbye to Fr. Schall. It was then that I came upon the idea of this book as a way to honor his life. I told Father Schall that I was planning to expand my essay into a book that captured in more detail my interactions with him. I humbly admit that this book draws inspiration from Mitch Albom's *Tuesdays with Morrie*. If imitation is the sincerest form of flattery, I credit *Tuesdays with Morrie* as inspiring the style of this book. But this book differs from *Tuesdays with Morrie* in several respects.

First, this book is about what Fr. Schall called "another sort of learning," instead of a learning process between a teacher and student. For Fr. Schall, to acquire education, it is often necessary *not* to do what the 'course' of studies in high school or college requires. Fr. Schall believed that two types of education might be pursued outside formal schooling: first, an education while we are making a living, as a lawyer, stock market analysis, entrepreneur, or engineer. The

---

[1] S. Hendrianto, S.J., *Saturdays with Fr. Schall: A young Jesuit on the older Jesuit's 90th birthday.* https://www.catholicworldreport.com/2018/01/23/saturdays-with-father-schall-a-young-jesuit-on-the-older-jesuits-90th-birthday/

second is the education that needs what Aristotle called leisure - space and time for questions that have little connection with business or earning money. For the latter, we want friends and we want to know what others, especially the ones who have more experience and lived longer, have held. Moreover, we must have good books, ones we have read, marked, and read again. If we intend to keep those books, then we must plan a dwelling to keep them, with shelves, rooms, and our own library system. The bottom line is this book is about a young Jesuit who experiences "another sort of learning" through friendship with an older Jesuit.

Second, this book is a combination of both the intellectual and spiritual life. Indeed, some parts of the book contain my intellectual exchange with Fr. Schall. This book is part of the search for knowledge, which according to Fr. Schall's favorite phrase, is the question of *what is*. But the intellectual life does not mean we are leaving our spiritual life behind or vice versa. As Father Schall said, the "openness we possess to all being is our grace and our blessing, what we have accepted because we receive, not make, our own being. When wonder is addressed by grace, we are. This is the spiritual life given to intelligent beings."[2] Indeed, the Catholic intellectual vocation invites us to integrate the intellectual life and spiritual life. Our lives must be grounded in Christ so that we can live more humanly and divinely. This book will not only include intellectual reflection, but also elements of the spiritual life.

---

[2] James V. Schall, S.J., *Another Sort of Learning* (San Francisco: Ignatius Press: 1988), 268.

Third, this book is about meditations on dying and living. By the time I met Fr. Schall in 2013, he was already 85 and had been dying for many years. He had cancer in early 2000s and underwent a long period of treatment. After a brief remission, the cancer recurred in 2010, causing him to have part of his jaw removed and replaced by a bone from his lower leg. On the top of that, he lost one of his eyes because of retinal detachment in 1989. There is no doubt that Father Schall led me to many reflections and meditations about death, but that was not everything. My interaction with him also involved meditations on living and breathing. Fr. Schall once said that if we find ourselves "living and breathing, it means that we keep on living our extended life that we began at conception."[3] As we only receive our life from the Giver of life, then our lives are a gift that makes us wonder about the Giver.

Fourth, this book shares the vocational journey of a young Jesuit becoming a priest of Jesus Christ, who is accompanied in this journey by an older Jesuit priest. When I met Fr. Schall in 2013, I was about to begin my regency assignment, a period in the Jesuit formation. From that time on, Fr. Schall accompanied me through my regency assignment and theological studies in preparation for priestly ordination. My friendship with Fr. Schall in many ways has strengthened my vocation, not only in that I want to be a priest like Fr. Schall, but more importantly, because he taught me a lesson on

---

[3] James V. Schall, S.J., "On Coming Back," Interview with Kathryn Jean Lopez, *National Review*, January 19, 2019, https://www.national-review.com/2019/01/father-james-schall-meditations-for-living/

what it means to be a priest of Jesus Christ. Our priesthood is centered on Jesus Christ; after all, a priest is just an instrument like the violin in the hands of a musician because Christ is the primary cause of grace. In other words, Christ is the musician who is playing the musical grace with his priests as instruments. Apart from that, Fr. Schall also reminded me that a priest needs to continue learning and studying for the sake of his pastoral work. If a priest simply puts studying in the rearview mirror and begins to work as if the loving care Christ's flock were opposed to the teaching of truths, it is a bit like a doctor having a proper bedside manner but little medical knowledge. A priest must have a good understanding of what he teaches first before he can tend the pastoral needs of the Christian people. At the end of the day, Fr. Schall taught me a lesson that studying is a kind of eighth sacrament for a priest.

Finally, all that happened in this book is based on my memory. But I have tried my best to be accurate and careful with my story. As Fr. Schall liked to say, "we are what we remember"[4] or in a similar spirit, "Tell me what you remember, and I will tell you what you are."[5] This book is about the stories of what I remember, and it implies the existence of time and the passing of my memories of Fr. Schall. Hopefully, by telling these stories, people can see who I am. Last but not least, Fr. Schall argued that the reason the elderly, such as himself, have a harder time remembering things is not due to a decline of memory. It is rather because their minds are filled with so

---

[4] James V. Schall, *On Remembering What We Know: An Illuminating Life*, address at the Faith and Reason Institute, in honor of Father John Navone, S.J., Gonzaga University, Spokane, April 24th, 2014.

[5] Ibid.

many things that it takes the brain, like a computer, time to find the item it is considering.[6] But you, my reader, can rely on my good memory to tell you my stories of Fr. Schall. I am grateful that God gives the gift of a good memory, and the memory of my 'computer' is still capable of processing many things. But at the end of the day, we Jesuits always pray what our founder St. Ignatius Loyola, taught us:

> Take Lord, and receive all my liberty, my memory, my understanding, and my entire will, all that I have and possess. Thou hast given all to me. To Thee, O lord, I return it. All is Thine, dispose of it wholly according to Thy will. Give me Thy love and thy grace, for this is sufficient for me.

Stefanus Hendrianto, S.J.
On the Feast of St. Ignatius of Loyola, 2020

---

[6] Ibid.

In the Beginning

On the Feast of St. Ignatius of Loyola

In 2013, Father Schall retired after many years of teaching at Georgetown University and moved to Los Gatos on the first day of spring. At the end of the spring of that same year, I left Chicago and flew to Santa Clara via San Jose. While Father Schall began his new mission of praying for the Church and the Society of Jesus (the Jesuit version of retirement), I was about to begin my regency assignment (a period in the Jesuit formation between philosophy and theological studies) at Santa Clara University.

Before I arrived at Santa Clara, I had heard of the legendary professor of government from Georgetown University, but I had not met him in person. I came across the name of James V. Schall for the first time in Fall 2011. At that time, I was just a naïve Jesuit Scholastic who had just pronounced vows of poverty, chastity, and obedience. After two years of Novitiate training and pronouncing my vows, I moved to study philosophy at Loyola University Chicago. Soon I found that philosophy is not an easy subject. Many philosophical writings contain abstract vocabulary and vague concepts, and I had difficulty finding a good mentor who could help me to learn basic philosophical concepts.

Nonetheless, I found a few good Jesuit teachers; one of them is the late Father Robert Araujo, S.J. In my first semester of philosophy study, I took a class with Fr. Araujo on Natural Law and Natural

Rights. In one of the sessions, Fr. Araujo assigned two articles written by Fr. Schall.[7] But again, as a naïve Jesuit scholastic who struggled with philosophical studies, it was difficult for me to grasp what
Fr. Schall wrote, and his articles did not leave a deep impression on
me at the time. My only impression about the assigned reading was
that Fr. Schall was one of the two Jesuits that we read in the class, the
other being Francisco Suarez, a 17th century Spanish Jesuit, philosopher, and theologian. I did begin to wonder about what was so special about James V. Schall, as we had to read his works along with
those of St. Thomas Aquinas, Suarez, and other great philosophers.

After my first semester was over, I soon began to forget the name
of James V. Schall. As I continued to struggle with my philosophy
studies, many things preoccupied my mind, and I did not bother to
think about this particular Jesuit any longer. Surprisingly, by the
grace of God, the situation got better by the end of my first year of
studies. I will explain what happened in the latter part of this book.
When I came back to Loyola Chicago in my second year, I had a
renewed interest in studying philosophy. It was then that I came
across the name of James V. Schall again in my seminar class on
Faith and Reason.

In the Faith and Reason seminar, we read the works of many
great thinkers such as Augustine, Aquinas, Abelard, Anselm, Newman, Chesterton, Gilson, and Maritain. One of my fellow Jesuits

---

[7] James V. Schall, "On Being Dissatisfied with Compromises: Natural
Law and Human Rights," 38 *Loyola Law Review* (#2, 1992), pp. 289- 309;
James V. Schall, "Natural Law & the Law of Nations: Some Theoretical
Considerations," 15 *Fordham International Law Journal* (#4, 1991- 92),
pp. 997-1030.

classmates, Kevin Embach, randomly mentioned that someone missing from the list was Fr. James V. Schall. Embach argued that we should read Fr. Schall's book, *The Order of Things*, which, according to him, was one of the best books that he had ever read. Kevin Embach was a compassionate and kind Jesuit, but he could be silly, and so I did not pay attention to his random suggestion.

After I arrived in Santa Clara at the end of Spring 2013, I began to hear the name of James V. Schall more often. Some members of the Santa Clara University Jesuit community were working at the Jesuit Curia, which was located in the same compound as the Sacred Heart Jesuit retirement center in Los Gatos. Those Jesuits shared how amazing the lunch table conversation was at the Sacred Heart Center, as many great Jesuits thinkers had retired there, such as Michael Buckley and James Schall.

On the Feast of St. Ignatius of Loyola in the summer of 2013, I finally met Father Schall in person when he and other retired Jesuits came to Santa Clara University for the celebration of our founder's feast. After a brief introduction, Fr. Schall asked me what I was going to do in my regency assignment at Santa Clara University. I told him that the plan was for me to teach in both the law school and political science department. Fr. Schall immediately asked what kind of courses I was going to teach. I told him that for the fall semester, I was going to teach a class on Human Rights theory. He immediately said, to my surprise, "I am not a human rights kind of person." Fr. Schall did not stop there, explaining that the notion of human rights is one of the most subversive ideas in the modern world, and further expressing that "human rights are a modern idea, stemming from

Hobbes." Well, here I was, a Jesuit, about to begin a teaching assignment on human rights, and now this legendary Jesuit immediately condemned the subject of my course! Trying to be polite, I asked him to elaborate more on his thoughts. Fr. Schall then explained that if we look back at world development in the last five decades, it becomes clear that the subversion of natural law has been carried out under the pretext of "human rights" as understood in particular by Hobbes. Thus, in many political societies across the world, we will find a common feature of abortion, homosexual living, euthanasia, and many other things logically connected with the notion of positive "human rights." So, according to Fr. Schall, when we hear the phrase "human rights," we almost invariably hear modern natural rights, which have no root but in will. I could see the point Fr. Schall made in his assessment of the danger of "human rights," but it was too late for me because I was stuck with my class on human rights beginning in about three weeks.

I read Hobbes when I was in philosophy studies at Loyola Chicago and I knew about his theory of the Leviathan and the law of nature. Still, I never heard about this theory on human rights. Curiously, I asked Fr. Schall whether he could elaborate further on his thoughts on Hobbes and human rights. Surprisingly, the conversation moved in a different direction, in which Fr. Schall asked, "Have you ever read Leo Strauss's famous essay, *Jerusalem and Athens*?" In all humility, I answered, "No." Fr. Schall then explained that Strauss argued that western civilization was composed of two essential elements: Jerusalem (the Bible) and Athens (Greek philosophy). According to Strauss, the modern project beginning with Hobbes and his contemporaries was an attempt to reject the core of this classical and biblical tradition. As a result, the questions of why man is man, what is his personal end, and happiness, became identified with what a man wants to do in the world. So the freedom that Hobbes and his contemporaries envisioned in the modern project depended solely on what the man wanted to be. Fr. Schall then explained that Strauss wanted to save humanity from the disastrous political consequences of the modern project by proposing that we must return to the classical political philosophy, by appealing to Athens and Jerusalem. "Do you know what his problem is?" asked Fr. Schall. Again, I had to admit that I had no clue what he is talking about. "Strauss had very little to say about Rome," stated Fr. Schall. Here Fr. Schall explained that Christianity as the third element (beside Athens and Jerusalem) had a unique contribution to Western civilization, but Strauss was mostly silent about Christianity.

Wow! I immediately thought that this short conversation was worth three credits of graduate courses. In the meantime, Fr. Schall noticed that the young Jesuit he was conversing with was not really well-versed in some political theories, and he gently said to me, "You still need to read a lot." He then recommended Strauss' famous essay and also some works of Eric Voegelin for a better understanding of the subject matter. Again, I had to humbly acknowledge that I had never heard the name of Eric Voegelin before. In my naiveté, I asked Fr. Schall what was perhaps a dumb question: "Father Schall, do you think the works of Martha Nussbaum are also good sources to understand this issue?" I mentioned Martha Nussbaum because I had read a few of her works in my philosophy study, and I knew that she had a particular interest in ancient Greek and Roman philosophy, as well as political philosophy. Fr. Schall then gently replied, "You can read her works, but be careful, because her thoughts are problematic." Honestly, I don't know what Fr. Schall thought of me in our first meeting; I hope that he did not think that the upcoming generation of Jesuits were a danger to the future of the Society of Jesus!

We had a pleasant conversation for the rest of the social time that evening. When the dinner was ready to be served, I did not sit at the same table with Fr. Schall and did not converse further with him that evening. I wished to spare myself the embarrassment of being asked more questions that I did not have answers to. After the dinner was over, Fr. Schall and other elderly Jesuits were escorted back to the retirement center in Los Gatos. I managed to say goodbye to him, and surprisingly, he invited me to visit him in Los Gatos if I would like to have a more extended discussion. "Come at any time," he said to me.

The First Saturday

Another Sort of Learning

After my first meeting with Fr. Schall on the feast of St. Ignatius of Loyola, I did not follow up on his invitation to come to visit him at Los Gatos. One of the main reasons was because I was too busy with my new life as a neo-regent, the term that the Jesuits used to describe men who are doing their regency assignment. Indeed, I was quite busy with teaching obligations to the Law School and Political Science Department. I also worked part-time in the advising office and assisted with campus ministry.

It was not until the second Saturday of January 2014 that I went to visit Fr. Schall in Los Gatos. I emailed Fr. Schall first about my plan to visit, he remembered me, and said that I could come at any time on that particular Saturday. I arrived in Los Gatos at around mid-morning and went to the nurse's station in the Retirement Center to check-in. I told the nurse that I was there to visit Fr. Schall and he knew that I was coming that morning. She called Fr. Schall's room and informed him that he had a visitor. She hung up the phone and told me that Fr. Schall would join me in the West Wing of the Infirmary. I waited for several minutes and then I saw Fr. Schall came out from the elevator. I greeted him and apologized for not visiting him earlier. He replied, "The weather is nice; why don't we walk outside?" So we walked around the Sacred Heart Retirement Center and tried to enjoy the warm, sunny California winter.

Our conversation soon turned to my work at Santa Clara University as Fr. Schall began to ask me about my experience of teaching. Honestly, I was trying to avoid the conversation about my Human Rights class in the previous semester. The course itself went quite well, but I did not want to talk about it for fear of Fr. Schall's potentially critical thoughts of it. I immediately shared the new class that I was about to teach on Religion and Politics in the Political Science Department's undergraduate program. Fr. Schall immediately asked me, "What kind of readings that you will assign to the students?" I told him that the focus on the class would be on the comparison between Catholicism and Islam and their relation to democracy. For the Catholicism part, I planned to assign Ken Himes' *Christianity and Political Order* as the primary textbook, along with some extra online reading materials. For the Islam part, I intended to assign online reading materials alone. Fr. Schall immediately asked me, "Have you thought about assigning your students Pope Benedict's Regensburg lecture?" When I replied, "no," he responded, "I highly recommend you assign the Regensburg lecture to your students."

I heard about Pope Benedict XVI's infamous Regensburg lecture when I was pursuing my doctoral studies at the University of Washington. But at that time, I was a naïve graduate student who was confined in my narrow academic field. Plus, I just came back to my faith about a year before and did not have the intellectual curiosity to read the lecture. I simply followed the news about the angry reaction in the Muslim world after the lecture, in which the Holy Father cited a passage unflattering to Prophet Mohammed. I read the address for the first time when I was pursuing my philosophy studies at Loyola

University Chicago. In my Faith and Reason Seminar, our professor asked us to read the lecture, but we mostly focused on the relationship between faith and reason in the lecture.

Though I had read the lecture, I decided to ask Fr. Schall to give me more insight into the address. Fr. Schall said, "I have published a book about it, so you can read it if you like." Nevertheless, Fr. Schall generously shared his insight about the lecture: first, he said that in the address, the Pope discussed the question of the relationship between the Old Testament and Greek philosophy. Fr. Schall pointed out that the Holy Father referred to St. Paul, who did not go to the East after his conversion, but instead, he went to Macedonia. Then Father Schall shared what to me was a stunning insight: that Christianity is not a religion but rather a revelation. Revelation is a reception of something that you try to understand and follow. Revelation is not something discerned directly by natural reason, but it is not contradictory to reason. Fr. Schall then explained that the early Christians did not address themselves to pagan religion, but rather to the Greek philosophers because they wanted to see whether what was being revealed to them was reasonable. Fr. Schall stated further that the entire western civilization was built upon the premise that revelation is corrected to reason and reason is open to the understanding of revelation.

I began to see why Fr. Schall highly recommended that I assign the Regensburg lecture to my students. It would help to clarify the meaning of religion and revelation, helping them to understand what religion meant before we discussed the connection between religion and politics. While I still had some lingering questions about

Fr. Schall's insight into the lecture, I intended to follow his suggestion and include the Address in my class.

Furthermore, Fr. Schall pointed out to me that the topic of Islamic Voluntarism that was raised by the Pope in the lecture was relevant to the topic of my class. In the Regensburg Lecture, the Pope cites the Muslim theologian Ibn Hazm, who states that "God is not bound even by his own word and that nothing would oblige him to reveal the truth to us. Were it God's will, we would even have to practice idolatry."[8] This citation signifies that there is a voluntarist God whose power is not limited even by the principle of contradiction and reason. Such a voluntarist God sees no problem with the use of violence in achieving certain objectives. Finally, Fr. Schall said that the main issue is whether Christianity and Islam do, in fact, worship the same God. If the voluntarist God is the true conception of Allah, then Christians do not worship the same God.

Though I knew the topic could be sensitive to my class discussion, I resolved to engage it. After all, what concerned Pope Benedict was not merely the voluntarism in Islam but also a similar mode of thinking in Christian thought. In his address, the Pope also raised his concern over voluntarism promoted by Duns Scotus, which led to the claim that we can only know God's *voluntas ordinata*. Scotus' proposition meant that in virtue of God's freedom, He could have done the opposite of everything He had actually done.

We had been walking for a little while around the compound of the Sacred Heart Center. We were slowly approaching the area near

---

[8] Regensburg lecture § 16

the old Novitiate winery. The Jesuits of the California Province originally built the old Novitiate winery in 1888. The winery was intended to help fund their new Novitiate. The young James Schall
when he was a Novice used to work in the old winery as all the novices did then. In 1986, the Jesuits shut down their Novitiate winery,
and in 1997, the winery underwent a new transformation, becoming
the Testarossa winery.

We stopped for a little while near the winery. I decided to question Fr. Schall on his thoughts about one of the reading materials in
my class. I had the reading materials in my backpack and showed it
to Fr. Schall. It was a working paper by a Brazilian scholar, Luiz Alberto Gómez de Souza, titled *Latin America and the Catholic
Church: Points of Convergence and Divergence (encontros e desen-
contros), 1960–2005*. The paper was published by the Kellogg Institute of International Studies at the University of Notre Dame. Fr.
Schall skimmed through the article quickly and pointed out to me
the citation from Hillary Belloc, "Europe is Faith and Faith is Europe." He said, "What Belloc said is precisely correct; why don't you
invite your students to reflect on this citation?" Fr. Schall stated further, "Go back to the Regensburg lecture; you will find that Benedict
addresses the question of what is Europe."

Again, I slowly understood what Fr. Schall told me earlier about
the foundation of western civilization in the Regensburg lecture. Europe is where the Old Testament, New Testament, and Greek and
Roman traditions melded together. Europe's unity was hammered
out in thought from the Fathers of the Church to Aquinas. But, as
Pope Benedict XVI explained in his lecture, the de-Hellenization

process of Europe and Christianity began with the Reformation and the rise of modernity.

Fr. Schall gave back the Alberto Gomez's paper to me. I understood him to imply that he did not recommend me to use the working paper for my class. Alberto Gomez cited Belloc as a denial of all claims of universality for the Christian religion (or, more specifically, Catholicism). His paper focused on Latin American Catholicism that emerged from the shadow of Europe and presented its visions for society and Catholicism. But for Fr. Schall, it was better to focus my class on the western civilization that has been under attack from all fronts.

Finding my reading list further 'humiliated' by Fr. Schall, I decided to ask him, "So Fr. Schall, apart from Regensburg lecture, are there any other readings or topics that you would recommend me to bring to my class?" Fr. Schall replied, "Do you know what pietas is?" Initially, I thought that Fr. Schall was referring to pieta of Michelangelo, a sculpture of the Virgin Mary holding the dead body of Jesus Christ on her lap and in her arms. It turned out that Fr. Schall referred to one of the chief virtues among the ancient Romans, rooted in religion and family life but also came to function as a political tool. In a nutshell, Fr. Schall explained that pietas encompass dutiful devotion towards family, state, and gods. Fr. Schall referred to Cicero, in which pietas was deeply imbedded in his philosophy of life, that the pietas entailed his duties to family and friends, the place of his birth, and the fatherland. Fr. Schall then said, "Why don't you introduce the idea of pietas to your students so that they learn about duty and respect for the natural order, politically and religiously?"

But soon, Fr. Schall realized that I was not well versed in the notion of pietas and ancient Roman philosophy. He then proposed a different suggestion.

"If you are not familiar with the concept of pietas, maybe you can ask your students to read of John Paul II's speech to the United Nations on Human Rights and Pope Benedict's speech to the UN, also on human rights."

I immediately replied, "But Fr. Schall, I thought that you are not a human rights person! Why suddenly would you recommend me to use the speeches of the two popes on human rights for my class?"

Fr. Schall smiled and replied to me, "Although JP II was quite critical to liberal political theory, he tried to infuse Christian substance to the liberal notion of rights." He said further, "If you want to learn more about JP II's use of the liberal rhetoric of rights with Christian substance, read the book of Tracey Rowland, *Culture and the Thomist Tradition*." I never heard the name of Tracey Rowland before, but I took note.

We spent many minutes walking outside the Sacred Heart Centre and Fr Schall looked tired. Although the Sacred Heart Jesuit compound was not a massive complex, a walk around the entire compound was tiring for an eighty-six year old man like Fr. Schall. I then told Fr. Schall that it was time for me to leave and let him take his rest. Fr. Schall invited me to stay a bit longer for lunch, but I decline the invitation, not wanting to impose upon his time. I said goodbye to him, and he said, "Come again next week if you have time, and maybe we can have lunch then." As I was driving back home to Santa Clara, I began to reflect on my encounter with Fr. Schall. I learned from someone, who had more experience and lived longer, on what he read and held true. This experience was another sort of learning that I would never experience from a formal classroom education.

The Second Saturday

On the Tragedy of the Library

On the next Saturday, I decided to come back to Los Gatos to visit Father Schall. As I did the week before, I went to the nursing station in the West Wing of the Infirmary and requested to see Fr. Schall. The nurse called Fr. Schall's room and then he came to see me. I was planning to stay for lunch, but I was hoping to further converse with Fr. Schall so I decided to come a little earlier before lunchtime. Father Schall looked at the clock and noticed that it would be a little while before lunch began, so he invited me to sit in a small TV room in the West Wing infirmary as we waited.

Fr. Schall began the conversation by saying, "Tell me a little bit yourself." Then I realized that we met twice already, but our conversation was mostly centered on my work as a regent at Santa Clara University. I told Fr. Schall that I was born and grew up in Indonesia and moved to the United States about ten years ago as a student. At that time, I came to the US to pursue my graduate studies at the University of Washington in Seattle. Upon the completion of my doctoral studies, I joined the Society of Jesus, the Oregon Province.

Fr. Schall rose from his chair, saying, "Speaking of Oregon Province, there is something that I want to show you." We walked across the building to the East Wing of the Infirmary. Fr. Schall then showed me a big empty room with a few empty bookshelves. It turned out the room used to be the library of the Sacred Heart Jesuit Center. Since the Jesuits wanted to expand the retirement home due to the influx of retired Jesuits, the Province decided to close their library in Los Gatos and planned to convert it into new infirmary rooms. The influx of retired Jesuits was due to a plan to combine the former California Province and Oregon Province. The Oregon Province decided to close their infirmary and retirement home in Spokane, Washington, and move the retired Jesuits to Los Gatos. Fr. Schall said, "They closed the library so that the Oregon men can have rooms to stay in this building." Fr. Schall stated further, "The closing of this library is a tragedy."

I was surprised to hear this, so I slowly and gently asked him to explain his statement. Fr. Schall continued, "When I moved here last year, I could easily find many classic books like Aquinas's *Summa* and Augustine's collected works. But now I don't have access anymore to those books." I began to understand that Father Schall's lament was understandable because after the library was closed, he had nowhere to go to check out the great works.

But Father Schall's lament did not end there. He continued, "Barbarians did not know about books, so they destroyed the libraries. We have many men today who are supposed to know about books, but they also destroy the libraries." Father Schall explained that every book, even the terrible ones, originated from reason and were a product of civilization. So destroying a library can be interpreted as a sign of the destruction of reason and civilization.

We were still standing in the empty library room when Fr. Schall asked me, "How is your personal library." Honestly, I, too, had 'destroyed' my library, which I admitted to Fr. Schall. When I finished my doctoral program at the University of Washington, I had collected around at least ten large boxes of books. But when I entered the Jesuit Novitiate in Portland, Oregon, we were only allowed to bring ten books. So I donated some of my books to the University of Washington Suzallo Library. The remainder of my books went to friends' homes. After I pronounced my perpetual vow as a Jesuit, I could not reclaim those books immediately, as I was moving to Chicago to study philosophy and did not have sufficient room. As time went on, my friends could no longer house my books, so they were either thrown away or donated.

This was not the first tragedy of the library in my life. When I left Indonesia for my graduate studies, I left an extensive collection of books with my sister, some books with my cousin, and some books with my friend. Again, the same thing happened. I was away for too long, and they could not keep my books any longer. My sister moved to a new apartment and did not wish to move books, so I asked her to donate them. My cousin closed his business and threw away the books that I left in his shop. The books left with a friend did not survive his home renovation. Tired of losing so many books, I decided to stop collecting books or having a personal library. When I finished my philosophy studies at Loyola Chicago, I decided to sell my books or leave them to the house library. By the time I moved to Santa Clara University, I had only two small boxes of a few essential books.

After listening to the tragedy of my private library, Father Schall said, "You must make it a priority to rebuild your library." Father Schall continued, "A personal library will assist you in your intellectual journey." Fr. Schall pointed out that personal libraries are composed of books that we have read again and again. With a private library, we can quickly go back and look up something when we have to deal with a problem or controversial issue.

Father Schall then stopped the conversation about the library and asked me, "What time is it now?" It was close to noon. "Let's go to the dining room for lunch now," he suggested. So we went to the dining room on the second floor. I sat with Father Schall and some other retired Jesuits at a large table. We did not have any further private conversation as we were seated among many Jesuits. After lunch, I said goodbye to Father Schall and drove back to Santa Clara. While we did not spend much time in private conversation that day, Father Schall's story and encouragement to build a personal library sunk into my head. His words encouraged me to re-build my private library. I knew that within the Jesuit life, building and keeping a private library was challenging due to the fact that we are transferred every two to three years and often, our accommodations lacked the space necessary to house books. Yet I determined to do so as a prerequisite to success as Father Schall suggested.

The Third Saturday

On Being Post-Indonesian

I came back to Los Gatos the following Saturday, close to lunchtime. Fr. Schall asked me to go directly to the dining room. In the dining room, he introduced me to his retired Jesuits companions as a man from Indonesia who entered the Oregon Province, who obtained his Ph.D. from the University of Washington, and was currently teaching at Santa Clara University. I felt a little bit uncomfortable, but let Father Schall introduce me as if he were proud of a poor Jesuit regent like myself.

We did not have a chance to have a private conversation as we sat at the big table with a few other Jesuits. After lunch, Father Schall suggested we walk outside again. We proceeded to the Grotto, where Father Schall asked, "Tell me more about Indonesia." Honestly, I didn't know where to begin because Indonesia is part of me. I have a hate and love relationship with my home country. Should I tell Father Schall of the many terrible things about Indonesia? I was not eager to share many good things about Indonesia as I felt reluctant to promote a country I had left behind. Partly because I disliked what the military regime had done to the citizens and primarily, because I had many bad memories of growing up as a 'second class citizens' in Indonesia.

Realizing that I didn't know where to begin, Father Schall tried another opening. "I had a student who is an Indonesian. Do you know the Riady family? One of the Riady kids was my student in

Georgetown." The Riady family is one of the influential Chinese Indonesian families, especially in the banking and financial sector. The patriarch of the family, Mocthar Riady, started a bicycle shop at the age of 22 and went on to build a successful banking empire under the banner of Lippo Group. Today Lippo Group's business empire includes real estate, retail, healthcare, media, and education. The heir apparent of the Lippo Group Empire, James Riady, was infamously involved in one of the biggest campaign finance scandals in US history. In 2001, James Riady pleaded guilty to conspiracy related to illegal campaign contributions to the 1996 Democratic Presidential campaign. James Riady also admitted that he made millions of dollars in illegal campaign donations to Democratic presidential and congressional candidates dating to 1988, including hundreds of thousands of dollars to Clinton's first presidential campaign in 1992.

For some reason, I got confused between the Riady family and another influential Chinese family in Indonesia, the Wanandi family. I replied to Father Schall, "Of course I know the family, they were the supporters of the military regime; Jesuits educated them, and even one of the brothers is a Jesuit priest." Fr. Schall replied, "Are they Catholic? I thought that they were evangelical Protestant." I said, "Oh yes, they are a Chinese Indonesia Catholic family." Then I explained the influence of the family in Indonesian politics. Jusuf Wanandi, the eldest of the Wanandi Brothers, is a lawyer and politician, who was an adviser to the General Suharto military regime in the 1970s and 1980s, and he was the Vice General Secretary of the Suharto's political party, Golkar. Sofyan Wanandi, Jusuf's immediate younger brother, is the family businessman, who made his fortune through his close association with Suharto's private assistants and military connection. Later, Sofyan Wanandi emerged as one of the business leaders in Indonesia. The youngest brother, Markus Wanandi, is a Jesuit priest, but there was a rumor that at some point, he played a pivotal role in undermining the role of the Catholic Church in East Timor during the Indonesian occupation.

Father Schall seemed confused to hear my story because it didn't seem to fit the family story of his former student. But as we were walking back toward the Sacred Heart Center building, I realized that I had confused the Wanandi family and the Riady family. I apologize, "Sorry Fr. Schall, I take it back what I said to you earlier; yes you are correct that the Riady family is an evangelical Protestant family. I got confused with a different influential Chinese family in Indonesia." Fr. Schall then teased me that his memory was still better than mine even though he is much older. "I heard that the Riady family has their own university," said Father Schall. Indeed, the Riady family established a Christian university, Universitas Pelita Harapan in Indonesia. "My former student is teaching at the university right now," he informed me. It turned out that Father Schall's former student was the third-generation crown prince, John Riady. He obtained his bachelor's degree in political science and economics from Georgetown University. He later earned an MBA from the Wharton School of Business and a JD from Columbia University Law School. While it was true that John Riady was listed as a professor of law at Pelita Harapan Law School, he was not merely an academic. He was in charge of leading the Lippo Group's effort to go digital and supervise the creation of the e-payment platform and later, he assumed the position of CEO of the property developer

Lippo Karawaci, the heart and soul of the $8 billion Lippo Group business empire.

I then said to Fr. Schall, "Well, Father Schall, the Indonesian that you knew is the crown prince of Indonesia's biggest family business empires; I hope that you won't mind being friends with a poor Chinese Indonesian like me." "Do you have Chinese ancestry?" asked Father Schall. I then explained my family history.

I grew up in a Chinese working-class family in Indonesia. Three generations of my family are mineworkers, from my great-grandfather to my father. They all worked in tin mining. I am the first person in my extended paternal family who graduated from college. Unlike John Riyadi, whose parents could send him to Georgetown, U Penn, and Colombia, my parents could barely pay for my high school education. I obtained my undergraduate, Master's, and doctoral degrees with scholarships from many different institutions.

"Your parents still alive?" asked Father Schall, to which I replied yes. "Do you talk with them often?" My honest answer was, "I talked with them a little bit, but not often." I then had to explain about my rocky relationship with my parents, especially my dad. My dad was a simple and kind man, but he could be an angry man when it involved his farm. My dad was operating a small-sized farm to support the family income as his work in the mining company was not sufficient to support the family. He wanted me to help on the farm a lot. I did try to help in different ways, but I was not good at the work. Part of the reason was that I was physically weak, but mostly because I preferred to spend my time reading rather than doing farm work. This caused my dad to frequently call me a "useless boy." My problem was that as a teenager with a sensitive heart, I did not know how to cope with a verbally abusive father. I responded by distancing my-self from him. As time went by, the gulf between us grew wider.

My dad had only a fifth-grade education, so it was hard for him to understand my academic pursuits. For him, I was just wasting my time with school and that it was my only skill. At some point, my dad said, "It will be better for you to be productive by cultivating our land rather than sitting at home reading books all the time."

When I told my dad that I wanted to be a priest and join the Jesuit Novitiate, he said, "You are one of the dumbest men in the world." He then compared me to one of the men in the village where I grew up. This fellow only had a primary education, but he ran a small fish farming business. In my dad's view, this man was much more successful than a Ph.D. like me, who would throw away my diploma and chose to join the Jesuits.

Father Schall said, "I am sorry to hear about that." Knowing that the topic of my relationship with my dad was a painful topic to dis-cuss, he then changed the subject. "Are there many Chinese Indone-sians?" I then explained that the Chinese population in Indonesia was only 3%, which is around 7.5 million.[9] However, the number of Chinese in Indonesia is the largest in terms of the number of over-seas Chinese per country. I continued to explain that, due to histor-ical-political reasons, the Indonesian government, especially under the New Order military regime (1966 -1998) treated Chinese Indo-nesians as second-class citizens. If you were Chinese, then you would face tremendous difficulties in enrolling in public schools, ap-plying to be civil servants, let alone joining the military or police.

---

[9] This information is based on the data of the 2010 census

Chinese Indonesians became scapegoats in situations of widespread discontent and social unrest. At the micro-level, the so-called native Indonesians always looked down upon us. One of the stereotypes about Chinese Indonesians is that they control the Indonesian economy. But I think that the truth is that there are about ten Chinese families who control the Indonesian economy, including the Riyadi family, but there are many poor, working-class Chinese like me.

"How do you feel being a Chinese Indonesian?" asked Father Schall. That was a difficult question as well, because for me, it was always a 'betwixt and between' situation. In Indonesia, I lived between two cultures, the culture of Chinese immigrants and Indonesian culture, although Indonesian culture itself is hard to define.

I was exposed to a little bit of our Chinese immigrant culture, but I didn't speak Chinese. Indonesian society and government always considered me as non-native even though my family had been residing in the country for four generations. In short, I was not fully integrated into or accepted by either cultural system; however, I also belong to both, although not fully.

After I came to the United States for my graduate studies, I felt that I became more Indonesian than I had been even in my own country. I could quickly identify myself as Indonesian in this foreign land without any need to clarify my Chinese ancestral roots. But things got more complicated after I joined the Society of Jesus. I joined the Oregon Province Jesuits, and there I was, the only Indonesian among a small number of Asians. The dominant culture in the province was still Euro-Caucasian, which was different than my culture. The issue before me was how I could identify myself as Chinese Indonesian while at the same time be an American Jesuit. For instance, some fellow Jesuits always introduced me to others as "a Jesuit from Indonesia." This introduction created some sort of confusion because many people thought either I had just come directly from Indonesia or they assumed that I was a member of the Indonesian Province of the Jesuits.

But having dealt with the identity issue for so long, I realized that I would not be able to possess a well-defined and established self-identity; I would always be in between both or often multiple identities. So, in the end, I identified myself as post-Indonesian. Being post-Indonesian did not mean I adhere to postmodern philosophy. Rather, there are a few things from post-modern thought that I used to help me to identify myself. One of the key elements of post-modernity is hybrid. While modernity – in its purest form, consists of the negation of the past, custom, tradition - post-modernity assumes that you can't escape the past. Time is not linear and it repeats. For modernity, novelty comes from creating out of nothing, but novelty in postmodern thought comes from recycling the past. To me, being a post-Indonesian means that I admit I can't escape from my past, but at the same time I can recycle my past and come out as a new person with a hybrid identity.

After hearing my long rant about my identity crisis, Father Schall responded as I would never imagine; "Maybe you need to re-read St. Augustine's *Confession*. St. Augustine was also struggling to search for an answer to who he was as a person. Even if Augustine's life doesn't resonate with you, it's always good to re-read classical literature like the *Confession*." Honestly, I didn't know how to respond to this suggestion. I wasn't sure if reading the *Confession* would help me deal with my identity issues. The last time I read the

Confession was when I was in the Novitiate, and I did not even finish the whole book. Nor did I have a copy.

We ended our conversation on that note, and I said goodbye to Father Schall. On my drive home to Santa Clara, I considered that while I would be unlikely to reread the *Confession* immediately, what with my current busy schedule, I would take Fr. Schall's suggestion seriously and re-read it during one of my retreats.

The Fourth Saturday

On Learning Philosophy
and Watching the Super Bowl in New Orleans

I went back to Los Gatos the following Saturday, but the nurse in the infirmary told me that Father Schall was out of town. It was my mistake to not email him first. However, when I returned the weekend after, Father Schall had returned.

On that particular Saturday, Fr. Schall invited me to sit at a private table so we could have a private conversation. During the lunch conversation, I asked Father Schall, where he went the previous week. It turned out that Father Schall was in New Orleans, giving a lecture at Notre Dame Seminary, which is located in the Carrollton section in the heart of Louisiana. Father Schall was invited as the Speaker for the Tenth Aquinas Lecture at the Notre Dame Seminary and he gave a talk titled, "On Openness to the Whole of Reality." In a nutshell, Father Schall spoke on the importance of the symbiotic relationship between philosophy and theology in Catholic thought.

Father Schall then asked me, "How was the experience of your philosophy study at Loyola Chicago?" With all the embarrassment, I then began to explain my experience of philosophy studies in the Windy City. I had to admit that we did not have a solid philosophy education at Loyola. I won't put all the blame on the Jesuits because a naïve Jesuit scholastic like myself is also responsible for the failure of our philosophy education. Some of us, including myself, came to our First Studies (the term that we often use to describe the philosophy program) with an attitude that we would do our best to avoid studying philosophy. For a man like me, partly because of my arrogance as a Ph.D. holder, I felt that there was no need for me to study an obscure subject like philosophy. Moreover, in my naivete, I could not understand the symbiotic relationship between philosophy and theology. While in the Novitiate, we were told that we had to study philosophy because it was a proper preparation for studying theology. I simply dismissed the suggestion. I argued that philosophy and theology were two different subjects and so there was no connection between the two, and why waste our time studying philosophy?

In my first year at Loyola Chicago, one of Jesuit philosophy professors urged us to take his class on metaphysics. Instead of taking a metaphysics class, I took a class on Philosophy of Action with a feminist professor. It turned out that it was one of the biggest mistakes I ever made in my graduate school history. I did not learn a lot from the class, and I did not perform well at the end of the semester. It was an awful tasting medicine that I had to swallow to realize that I had a disordered attachment to my pride in holding a Ph.D.

Father Schall then asked, "What did you learn then in philosophy? Did you learn Aristotle, Plato, and Aquinas?" Again, with embarrassment, I told Father Schall that my class on Classical Philosophy was elementary. I never had a class on Aquinas because the School did not offer any courses on his philosophy during my two years at Loyola. "It is a joke and a tragedy that you did not have a class on Aquinas," said Father Schall.

"Did anything good come out your philosophy studies?" asked Father Schall further. I replied yes because even under this mediocre philosophy program, I learned a lot during my First Studies. First, I had a few excellent classes, such as Natural Law & Natural Rights, Faith & Reason, and an excellent course on the Catholic Intellectual Revival of the 20th century. Second, my best philosophy education was mostly from outside the classroom. Through interactions with some Jesuit Fathers at the Jesuit Community in Loyola, either at the kitchen table or in private conversation, I learned a lot about philosophy.

God can also work mysteriously; the best moment in my study of philosophy came out from the class that my fellow Jesuits considered the worst class. In my second semester, we took a course on the History of Christianity, from Reformation to Modernity. The professor used a pedagogy that was a bit high-schoolish, and so many Jesuits were frustrated with the class. But it turned out this class was the best class for me in a unique way. As I did not learn a lot from the course, I had to teach myself about the subject matter. I ended up learning from a book that I consider saved my vocation, titled *The Theological Origins of Modernity* by Michael Allen Gillespie. Reading this book, I realized that the debates during the Reformation were philosophical debates; Martin Luther turned against Scholastic philosophy, which, according to him, was influenced too much by Aristotle. This experience is an 'aha moment' for me because, for the first time, I realized that philosophy and theology were interrelated.

Having heard my story, Father Schall said, "Well, at least, you learned something there and remember that education comes not only from the classroom." Then Father Schall recommended me to

use my time in regency at Santa Clara to study philosophy more rig-
orously. He also suggested perhaps that I could teach some philosophy courses at Santa Clara. Father Schall's suggestion of teaching
philosophy couldn't work for many different reasons. First, I had no
formal degree in philosophy; I only did the minimum requirement
of philosophy at Loyola, finishing the program without any formal
degree. At that time, I thought that I already had my Ph.D. and
didn't need another formal degree. But maybe it was a mistake because if I had a master's degree in Philosophy, I might have been able
to follow up on Father Schall's suggestion. But even if I had formal
credentials in Philosophy, there was only a small chance for me to
teach a philosophy class at Santa Clara University. The second reason was that Santa Clara University did not require students to take
philosophy classes any longer as part of their core curriculum. When
I came to Santa Clara University in 2013, the University had been
implementing a new core curriculum for several years. Under the
new core curriculum, the philosophy course requirement was replaced with a so-called new course called Culture and Ideas. This
new requirement was a two-course themed sequence that could be
anything from Cultures of Islam, Nietzsche, Women in Transna-
tional Perspective, or many other courses that had nothing to do
with philosophy. Listening to my story, Father Schall replied, "It's
very sad to hear that they are not teaching students philosophy any
longer."

I knew it was hard for a man like Fr. Schall to hear this reality
about a Jesuit sponsored university. Father Schall had his early education at Santa Clara University, but at that time, the curriculum was
pretty much aligned to the vision of Jesuit education under the *Ratio*

Studiorum, which included the study of scripture and Thomas Aquinas as the principal author for theological texts. Aristotle was prescribed as the standard subject for a professor of philosophy. Of course, Latin and Greek were also taught to the students. But much had changed since the time Father Schall studied at Santa Clara University.

I did not want to end our lunch conversation on a sad note like that. I switched the topic of conversation, asking, "Father Schall, did you do anything else when you were in New Orleans?" He answered, "I watch the Super Bowl in the Jesuit community." I was not completely surprised to hear about it because from reading his book, *Reasonable Pleasure*, I knew that Father Schall was indeed a sports fan, as he believed that sports or watching games are similar to the contemplation of the highest things. Moreover, Fr. Schall found that sports could help us to reflect on revelation. The fact of the matter is that in every sports game or competition, there are a few winners and the rest are losers. The revelation was designed with losers in mind because revelation is filled with words like salvation, repentance, and forgiveness.

"Did you watch the Superbowl?" asked Father Schall. I replied, "I just watched it a little bit." It was the Superbowl XLVIII championship game between the Denver Broncos and the Seattle Seahawks, in which the Seahawks defeated the Broncos 43–8. Although I had been residing in the country for ten years, I was not fully immersed in American sports culture, especially football. Though I lived in Seattle for five years and considered the Emerald City as my adopted home, I didn't have any allegiance to the Seahawks. Father Schall had plenty of reasons to convince me why I should watch the Super-bowl. But in the end, Father Schall did not push me to loving American football. He knew that a post-Indonesian like myself might need some time to learn and to enjoy American sports culture.

We finished our lunch, and then I said goodbye to Father Schall. I did not mention my plan to come back next Saturday. But I guessed that he knew that I might go back next Saturday to see him at the Sacred Heart Center.

The Fifth Saturday

On Jacques Maritain and Saul Alinsky

I came back to Los Gatos on the following Saturday, but the nurse in the infirmary told me that Father Schall was on his retreat and so he would not accept any guests. Every Jesuit makes an annual 8-day silent retreat, and Father Schall was making his annual retreat in Los Gatos. I went back home and planned to return on the following Saturday. The nurse told me that Father Schall had been on the retreat for a couple of days, and so I presumed that Father Schall would finish his retreat the following Saturday. When I arrived in the Sacred Heart Center the next Saturday, the nurse in the infirmary told me that Father Schall left the premises the day before, and he would spend his weekend in Ben Lomond. Ben Lomond is a small town located in the north of Santa Cruz; it is the home to Big Basin Redwoods, California's oldest state park. Santa Cruz itself is a colorful mix of a college town, beach town, and cultural center. It is famous for its boardwalk, wide sandy beaches, and beach amusements. I was wondering why Father Schall would spend his weekend in a place that attracted hippies, yuppies, and families alike. It turned out that Father Schall's nephew and his family lived in the area and he wanted to spend time with them.

Again, I went back home without meeting with Father Schall, so I decided to email him and let him know of my next intended visit. Father Schall emailed me back and said that he would be in Rhode Island the coming weekend, but I could come the Saturday after. I was surprised to hear that Father Schall was already traveling out of town again; he just got back from his trip to New Orleans in January, and now he was traveling again to the East Coast.

It wasn't until the second Saturday of March that I had a chance to see him again in Los Gatos. I came around lunchtime and Father Schall immediately asked me to go with him to the dining room. We sat at a big table with some other retired Jesuits.

"Father Schall, what did you do in Rhode Island last week?" I asked him. He replied, "I was attending the Annual Conference of the American Maritain Associations in Providence College." An elderly Jesuit who sat across the table joined our conversation, saying, "Do you know that Jim is a famous person? He was awarded an Oscar in a lifetime achievement." I knew that this elderly Jesuit was joking, but his joke did not make sense to me. It turned out that Father Schall received the Lifetime Achievement Award from the American Maritain Association at their annual conference at Providence College. The elderly Jesuit posed another question to Father Schall, "Did you feel good after receiving the lifetime achievement award?" Father Schall replied, "Yes, I am feeling good because I am still alive." I appreciated that Father Schall was making a joke that the 'lifetime' achievement award was given to a living person. In other words, he wouldn't receive such an award if he was already dead.

We spent the rest of the time at the lunch table discussing random items with some other elderly Jesuits. After we finished the meal, Father Schall invited me for a walk. During our walk, I immediately asked him, "Father Schall, I want to ask you about Maritain. Why was he such good friends with Saul Alinsky?"

"Where did you hear about that?" asked Father Schall.

"I read about it in Ralph McInerny's book's *The Very Rich Hours of Jacques Maritain.*"

"I am impressed to hear that you read McInerny's book. It's one of the books that I highly recommend people to read."

Father Schall knew my reading list was quite limited and so he was surprised to hear that I had read one of his favorite books. I told Father Schall that I read the book during my philosophy studies at Loyola University Chicago. I randomly picked the book from the library for my spring break reading in 2013. I remember that I couldn't put the book down during my spring break in the Jesuits' villa house in Michigan City. The only moment I put down the book was when I watched the Big East regular-season title Women's Basketball game between the Notre Dame Fighting Irish and U Conn Huskies, in which the Fighting Irish won in a triple-overtime thriller.

I read some of Maritain's works in my courses, such as Natural Law, Faith and Reason, and the 20th Century Catholic Intellectual Revival. So I wanted to know more about the life of Jacques and Raissa Maritain. One of my professors who added to my interest in the Maritains was Father Stephen Schloesser, S.J., who taught a class on the 20th Century Catholic Intellectual Revival. Nevertheless, when I told Father Schloesser that I read McInerney's book, he was quite skeptical and said, "The book is weird like McInerney, who was very weird." Father Schloesser then recommended I read a book titled *Jacques & Raïssa Maritain: Beggars for Heaven* by a French historian, Jean-Luc Barré. But I found Barré's book boring and never finished it. It was a very different experience compared to my reading of McInernery's *The Very Rich Hours of Jacques Maritain*.

Having listened to my story about the books on the Maritains, Father Schall replied, "There is a mystery of how our mind speaks through reading a book." In Father Schall's view, the same book can move someone's will and understanding differently than it would another's, and so it was not a surprise that I got nothing out of reading Barre's book, while Schoelleser was on fire after reading it. Similarly, I could be excited about reading McInerny's book, while Schloesser found it "weird."

Having realized that we had gone off the rails of our conversation, I repeated my question, "So Father Schall, is that true that Jacques Maritain was a good friend of Saul Alinsky?"

"Oh yeah, he loves an activist like Alinsky," said Father Schall.

"But I don't understand how a gentle and soft-spoken Thomist like Maritain could consider a rough, agnostic Jew like Alinsky his very closest friend. Did they have something in common?"

"Have you ever read Maritain's *Man and the State*?" asked Father Schall.

"I never read the whole book and only a few chapters of it."

"You should take your time to read it if you want to understand Maritain better. In that book, he wrote that democracy needs a prophet and he considered Saul Alinsky such a prophet."

Father Schall continued, "He also argued in that book that the political order must be conceived in the context of subsidiarity, leaving authority to the lowest level possible. Maritain found that Alinsky's community organizations and neighborhood councils were the perfect embodiment of subsidary."

"Still, I don't understand how a man like Maritain didn't see that Alinsky's tactics and strategies were very similar to the Communists' strategies."

"Oh, he did not see it in that way; for Maritain, Alinsky was very Thomistic."

"I don't know that Alinsky was a Thomist."

"Alinsky is not a Thomist, but for Maritain, he was a practical Thomist." Father Schall explained that Maritain saw Christian contemplation as not confined to the intellectual sphere alone but was found in faith that can be translated into action, in virtue from the abundance of love. The action then springs from the abundance of contemplation.

"Well, it sounds like Jesuit contemplation in action," I said to Father Schall.

"Don't you know that St. Thomas had a great influence on Saint Ignatius and his companions?"

"Oh, I never heard about that."

"What did they teach you in the Novitiate?"

To cover my embarrassment over what we did not learn in the Novitiate, I switched the subject by asking Father Schall to explain more about Maritain's contemplation in action within the Thomistic framework. Father Schall pointed out that Maritain found contemplation in action in St. Thomas Aquinas, who saw the Incarnation, both in reality and symbolism, as giving meaning to the lives of action that spring out of contemplation, which is filled with abundant love and generosity.

Father Schall explained further that for Maritain, the Incarnation, in the sense of God becoming man, was more important than man searching for God in philosophical contemplation. Maritain saw the problem in Western philosophy as the progeny of Greek philosophy, which tends to focus on contemplation and not see the world condition. It neglects the premise that superabundant contemplation would manifest into superabundant action. In sum, Maritain's theoretical position is that Christian contemplation must be translated into action while remaining contemplative. In other words, Christian contemplation not only includes the philosophical mind but also practical action.

"It seems to me that Maritain was adopting the Marxist axiom that the philosophers only interpret the world, but they do not know how to change it. So, do you think that he is a closet Marxist?" I asked Father Schall.

Father Schall smiled and replied, "Maritain did see the slowness of the coming of Kingdom of God, but he did not look to establish a paradise on earth like Marx wanted to do. His contemplation in action is merely an effort to put the good revealed to us by God in our temporal world."

"Father Schall, I have another question… as the recipient of the Maritain Lifetime Achievement Award, you are also critical of Maritain's philosophy; why then did you dedicate your time to study about this man?"

Father Schall smiled again and replied, "Maritain was a philosopher open to all branches of philosophy. While he remained loyal to the Aristotelian-Thomistic tradition, he also knew Descartes and Rousseau. If you read him for a long time, you will see his capacity to indicate one thing that leads to everything else. He discussed art with politics, politics with metaphysics, philosophy with the bible. He was a lover of truth and goodness."

We finished our conversation on that note; I said goodbye to Father Schall and headed back home to Santa Clara. I told him that I would let him know when I would come to visit him next. Father Schall said that he wouldn't be traveling for a while, and I could visit him at any time. While driving home, my mind wandered to my conversation with Father Schall about Maritain. I still had many questions about this man; his contribution to the Catholic Church and if his philosophy would bring both positive and negative effects to the Church. His friendship with Saul Alinsky was still puzzling to me. Was that possible for two persons with totally different worldviews to be good friends? It reminded me of the friendship between a conservative intellectual, Robbie George, and a radical Democrat like Cornell West. They were indeed an odd ideological couple, but they seemed to share a deep friendship. Friendship is, indeed, a mystery.

The Sixth Saturday

Finding a Red Book in the Redwood Monasteries

The Winter quarter went by quickly and I hadn't had a chance to visit Father Schall, not only because of academic obligations but also because of my work in campus ministry. Apart from teaching, I was also assisting at Campus Ministry. One of the upcoming projects was the alternative spring break. I had volunteered to be a co-leader of a group that would visit the Cistercian Nuns at the Our Lady of Redwood Monastery at Whitehorn in Northern California. I emailed Father Schall and let him know that I wouldn't be able to visit him until after the Spring break. He simply replied, "I will be here whenever you want to come to visit."

We left the campus right after the students finished their final exams. It was a five-hour to drive from Santa Clara to the Monastery. An exciting piece of history about the Monastery is that Thomas Merton visited the Monastery in May 1968 in his search for a new hermitage site. His trip to Redwood Monastery was part of his extended trips from the Abbey of Gethsemani, his monastic home in Kentucky, before he left for his Asian journey in Fall 1968.[10] Eventually, Merton died in Bangkok on December 10, 1968 while he was attending an Interfaith Conference.

During our visit to the Monastery, I had the privilege of staying in the same room where Merton stayed forty-six years earlier. It was

---

[10] Between May 16 and October 15, when he left for Asia, Merton visited California, New Mexico, Washington D.C., Chicago and Alaska.

a simple room, with a single bed, a desk, and chair. The room had probably not changed a lot since 1968.

Our activities during the visit pretty much followed the rhythm of the monastic life, to pray and to work. We woke up early in the morning, around 4:30 AM and joined the Sisters for morning meditation, followed by Lauds (Morning Prayer). The nuns chanted the Psalms, and most of us tried to follow them. After the morning prayer we joined the Sisters for Mass, which was celebrated by Father Morris who served as the chaplain for the Monastery. During the day, we help the Sisters with most of their communal works, packaging the honey, cracking the walnuts, gardening, and cleaning the Monastery. Perhaps the biggest challenge for the students-participants was that they must remain in silence. We ate in silence and performed the communal work in silence and stayed silent for the rest of the day, except for recreation or a group discussion. We usually closed the day with Compline (night prayer) at around 8 PM and went to bed afterward.

The experience at the Redwood Monastery reminded me of the book I read in the Novitiate, *Walking in the Spirit,* by the late Father Joseph Conwell, S.J. What a coincidence that Father Conwell died just a few weeks before our trip to the Redwood Monastery! In the Preface of the *Walking in the Spirit*, Father Conwell shared his encounter with a founding member of the Redwood Monastery, Sister Cecilia W. Wilms. They had built a close collaboration for many decades, even producing one book together titled, *Impelling Spirit*. Father Conwell explained how Sister Wilms helped him to understand the difference between his Jesuit vocation and her monastic vocation. One day Sister Wilms to Father Conwell, "For you, this book is part of your mission; for me it is a job that earns money for my support." This statement helped Father Conwell to realize that Sister Wilms spoke as a hermit whose calling was to pray, and the book project that she took during her leave from the Monastery was to support for her life of prayer. She needed to earn her living expenses so that she could pray.

My visit to the Redwood Monastery helped me also to reflect on my Jesuit vocation in terms of how profoundly different our charisms are. Here I was, a Jesuit Scholastic, who had no desire to be a monk. As much as I love the silence and the rhythm in the Monastery, I still much preferred to live the Jesuits' "mixed life." Interestingly, Father Conwell argued that the Jesuits' idea of contemplative action originated from St. Thomas Aquinas' notion of *mixed life*, which consists of both action and contemplation.[11] Nevertheless, while Aquinas was talking about *mixed life*, which consists of contemplation and action through preaching or teaching, the First Jesuits expanded the action to include many other activities as well, such as feeding the poor and helping the sick.[12]

But the highlight of my visit was finding one of the best books I ever read. On one afternoon, I was looking around the Monastery library and I found a slender book with a red cover titled, *The Intellectual Life: Its Spirit, Conditions, and Methods* by a French Dominican priest cum philosopher, Antonin-Gilbert Sertillanges, O.P. The

---

[11] Conwell, *Walking in the Spirit*, 158.
[12] Ibid., 229.

man who wrote the foreword for the book was no other than James V. Schall.[13] Father Schall wrote in the preface:

> I would put *The Intellectual Life* on the desk of every serious student and most of the unserious ones.... Its very position on our desk or shelves is a constant prod, a visible reminder to us that the intellectual life is not something alien, not something that we have no chance, in our way, to learn about.[3]

Father Schall's preface was quite intriguing, so I borrowed the book from the Monastery library and read it during my stay. In a nutshell, Sertillanges believes we can lead a productive intellectual life if we manage to keep one or two hours a day for the serious pursuit of higher things. Sertillanges did not ask us to give up our daily lives and devote ourselves full-time to the intellectual apostolate, like St. Thomas Aquinas did, but he teaches us to organize our lives so we can acquire a good intellectual foundation and spend the rest of our days building on this solid foundation. In this way, Sertillanges teaches us about habits, about discipline, productivity, and truth.

Having read the book, I could not wait to go back to Santa Clara and see Father Schall. I wanted to share with him my experience of finding a treasure in the Redwood Monastery. We only had one week of spring break and by the time we came back to Santa Clara

---

[13] Sertillanges *La Vie Intellectuelle* was originally published in 1921. The Catholic University of America Press published the book in English in 1987 and reprinted the book in 1998 with a new foreword by Father James V. Schall, S.J.

on Sunday, the Spring quarter would start immediately. I had to wait until the weekend to visit Father Schall.

On the first Saturday of April, I visited Father Schall in Los Gatos. I immediately shared with Father Schall my finding. Father Schall was glad to hear that I found the book on my own and apologized that he did not recommend me to read the book earlier. He told me that the book would have a lasting, concrete effect on me. "If you follow Sertillanges' simple prescription, it will enable you to build an intellectual life," said Father Schall.

I then shared with Father Schall my frustration in the past months and new insight after reading *The Intellectual Life*. I felt that I was quite busy with my teaching obligations in Law School and Political Science. Besides, I also worked part-time in the advising office and assisted at campus ministry. My daily schedule usually began with morning prayer, then was followed by exercise, breakfast, and reading newspapers. By the time I finish my morning routine, it was already around 9 AM or so. I tried to do some work afterward but I only had less than three hours to work before lunch. Or, if I had a class to teach in the morning, my morning was consumed with teaching and office hours. After the lunch break, I only had four extra hours to work until I had to take another break for daily Mass. I became frustrated with my daily schedule and felt that life was so difficult with teaching obligations and other responsibilities. My frustration partly stemmed from the fact that, with limited windows to work, I did not have enough time to read or write for a publication. But after reading *The Intellectual Life*, I realized that the real issue was not because I had too much work to do, which was true, but more because I had trouble building order in my life.

Father Schall then reminded me of what Sertillanges said in the book about the cycle of our day: fresh morning, burning midday, and evening decline. "When you only have a few productive hours, morning deserves to be the preference," said Father Schall. He then recommended I use my morning for reading, writing, and contemplation. He said further, "Don't waste your time reading the newspaper in the morning; you won't miss anything if you don't read it."

Before we went for lunch, surprisingly, Father Schall asked me to take some books from his room. I was bit puzzled as to why he decided to let go of some of his personal books. He said to me, "When I am gone, they will throw these books away, so why don't you take them with you now?" I was very excited that I found a 'treasure' of the intellectual life from Father Schall's personal collection. After lunch, I said goodbye to Father Schall. Before I drove back to Santa Clara, Fr. Schall reminded me to read my copy of *The Intellectual Life* and start building the habits of diligent work as prescribed by Sertillanges. I told him I hoped to come back to visit him soon.

The Seventh Saturday

On Plato at the Googleplex

The Spring quarter had been a frustrating one for me. The undergraduate class taught in Political Science had been a challenging class to manage. Some students in my class were those who barely attained a minimum GPA to graduate and they took the class merely to graduate. Some other students were challenging to deal with: they either disrespected me as a professor or rebelled against me. For my part, I became frustrated and impatient with those students.

It was already early May when I finally had a chance to visit Father Schall in Los Gatos. As usual, I came to the West Wing of the Infirmary and checked in at the Nursing Station. Surprisingly, the nurse on duty told me that I was not allowed to visit Father Schall in his room because there was a new directive from the Superior of the Retirement Community. It turned out that some lay visitors spent too much time with certain retired Jesuits in their rooms. I tried to convince the nurse that I was a Jesuit Scholastic and not a lay visitor. But the nurse refused to budge; instead she called Father Schall in his room and asked him to come down to see me.

Father Schall came out of the elevator a few minutes later. He invited me to sit in the small TV room near the West Wing Infirmary. Father Schall asked me about my work as a regent at Santa Clara. I shared with Father Schall about my disastrous class.

"It seems that the troubled students tend to gravitate towards you," said Father Schall. The statement was a bit puzzling to me because I didn't know why those students would be attracted to my class. Maybe because I was a young professor and they thought I would give them an easy pass, or I could be easily intimidated. Father Schall explained his earlier statement, saying, "The problem is that you are new and so the students do not know you. If you already had a good reputation as a professor, many students would enroll in your class and you would have much better quality students."

Father Schall then switched the topic of conversation by asking me, "What books have you been reading lately?" I told Father Schall I purchased a copy of *The Intellectual Life* and re-read it. I had also just ordered a book titled *Plato at the Googleplex: Why Philosophy Won't Go Away*. I wanted to read and learn more about Plato because I did not have a solid foundation on Plato from my philosophy study at Loyola Chicago. Father Schall immediately responded, "If you want to learn about Plato, read all of the dialogues of Plato. Don't waste your time reading random secondary literature about Plato."

"The whole dialogues? It may take some time for me to finish those dialogues."

"My students read all of the dialogues in one semester, so it's doable," explained Father Schall.

Father Schall then encouraged me by sharing his personal story. Father Schall explained to me that it's never too late to learn about Plato because he came to appreciate Plato rather late in life. It turned out that Father Schall's earlier thought on Plato was negative due to the influence of his mentor Father Charles McCoy, who saw in Plato the incipient errors of modern thought.

Having heard Father Schall's journey with Plato, I said, "I once read that Plato is the one who laid the groundwork for totalitarianism." Here I was referring to Karl Popper who argued that Plato's vision in the *Republic* was in part inspired by Sparta as an exemplar of the closed society, which laid the groundwork for totalitarianism. "You need to be careful with such a proposition," Father Schall replied. Father Schall explained that while it is true that every intellectual aberration can find its roots somewhere in Plato, the opposite is also exactly true, that most of what is good and profound also has its roots in Plato.

I tried to switch the topic of conversation by asking Father Schall, "I do understand that philosophy is important for a priest's learning and understanding of theology, but I wonder if learning Plato will be helpful for our priestly ministry?"

"Do you pray the Office?" asked Father Schall.

"I just pray the Lauds, Vespers, and Compline but not the whole Office."

I was not an ordained Minister yet, so I didn't have an obligation to pray the whole Office. Nevertheless, since our time in the Novitiate, we had been taught to pray Lauds and Vespers. When I was in the Novitiate, praying the Office was one of my least favorite activities. At that time, I thought that praying the Office was boring and monotonous. Surprisingly, after I finished the Novitiate and moved to philosophy studies, I began to miss praying the Office and slowly I started to pray it by myself.

Having heard my story, Father Schall commented, "That's because you have less resistance within your heart." He was right; I didn't like to pray the Office in the Novitiate because there was some resistance within my heart. Nevertheless, grace had slowly penetrated my heart and opened it to pray the Office.

Father Schall then moved back to the point that he wanted to make about praying the Office. He pointed out that one will notice before each Psalm in the Office, there is a brief passage from the New Testament or the Church's Fathers. These short passages point out Christ's life – His Birth, Passion, Death, and Resurrection. Here we find the Old Testament as understood in the light of the New Testament.

I was trying to follow Father Schall's chain of argument and wondered where he was going with his points. I did not have to wait for too long as Father Schall explained, "Augustine, Aquinas, and others read the works of pagan philosophers like Plato and Aristotle in the same manner, to point to the truth of Catholicism." Father Schall noted that when St. Augustine wrote *The City of God* (*De Civitate Dei*), he was referring to Plato's *República* (*Republic*). Thus, *The City of God* is a Catholic reading of Plato's *Republic*. Father Schall pointed out further that Pope Benedict XVI or Joseph Ratzinger also did a Catholic interpretation of Plato's works on justice and the immortality of the soul in his brilliant encyclical, *Spe Salvi*.

"Have you ever read *Spe Salvi*?" asked Father Schall.

"Of course, and it has had a profound impact on my faith journey."

"I don't know what you read, but it's good to hear that the document had a significant impact on your life. Tell me about your experience with *Spe Salvi*."

I began to share my story. I grew up under the military dictatorship in Indonesia and the military presence was prevalent in our daily life. I went to the only Catholic high school in my town and it was in the outskirts of the city. The school was located near a military barracks and we had to pass the military barracks as the only way for us to go to the school. The problem was that military children continuously harassed and bullied the male students. They teased and taunted us, and sometimes hit and pushed us.

Moreover, I had also to struggle with the reality that I was Chinese Indonesian. Due to historical-political reasons, the Indonesian military treated Chinese Indonesians as second-class citizens. Chinese Indonesians became the typical scapegoat in situations of widespread discontent and social unrest. At the micro level, the so-called native Indonesian students always looked down upon us.

When I was in college, I joined the student movement and was involved in the struggle for democracy in Indonesia. We read some Marxists literature and those literature inspired us to fight against the military dictatorship in Indonesia.

Many of my friends were jailed, kidnapped, or even killed by the military regime. Eventually, General Soeharto resigned from the presidency after mounting pressure from the student protests.

During my years of political activism, I slowly abandoned my faith and stopped going to the Church. My deep conversion experience took place after I read *Spe Salvi*. In this document, I found the

Pope's criticisms of Marx's dictatorship of the proletariat quite convincing. Having read the *Spe Salvi*, I decided to re-embrace Catholicism. The conversion then helped me in the discernment of the religious life and eventually, my decision to enter the Jesuit Novitiate.

"What did you find in *Spe Salvi* so compelling?" asked Father Schall.

"With his revolution, Marx promises a new world that is free from injustice and suffering. But as Pope Benedict described, Marx's fundamental error is he thought that when the economy had been put right, everything else would automatically right itself. He forgot that men always remain men. Human personalities are very complex, and this complexity can't be changed by simply creating a good economy."

"Obviously you read and understand *Spe Salvi* quite well," said Father Schall. He added, "It's amazing that a document like *Spe Salvi* can change your heart and bring you back to the Church."

I immediately clarified the chronology of my conversion. While it was true that *Spe Salvi* was instrumental in my conversion, the process had started long before I read the letter. I left the student movement around 2001, and then I came to the United States in 2004. Within those three years, I had had several mini conversions. Pope John Paul II died in 2005 and was succeeded by Benedict XVI. Pope Benedict published *Spe Salvi* on November 30, 2007, and I read it in the winter of 2008. From the time I arrived in the US and read *Spe Salvi*, I already had many profound conversion experiences.

"Tell me more about your conversion stories," asked Father Schall.

"It's a long story, but I think that we should have lunch, as it's getting late. I can share the story later during our lunch."

We moved to the dining room and found all the tables already occupied. We could not find a private table and had to join other Jesuits. I did not feel comfortable sharing my conversion stories with people I did not know well. So I decided to postpone sharing the rest of my conversion story to Father Schall. Father Schall understood the situation, and we chatted with other Jesuits during lunch time. After lunch, I said goodbye to Father and promised to share my conversion story at my next visit.

As I was driving home to Santa Clara, I began to think about what I should do with *Plato at the Googleplex*. Based on my conversation with Father Schall, there was no point for me to read the book. Maybe I could just return it to Amazon since they had a good return policy. The question was whether returning an unwanted product is an ethical thing to do. I know that one of my fellow Jesuits, John Roselle, would condemn me if I returned the book because he believed that we should not treat Amazon like a grocery store. John Roselle had a good heart, but he was a scrupulous man. I remember a moment when we were together in Loyola Chicago. It was the last day of the final exam and we decided to see a movie to celebrate the completion of our studies. We watched Terrence Malik's movie *To the Wonder*. I bought a student ticket and John immediately condemned me because he thought it was unethical since I just finished my last exam a few hours earlier. But the graduation was still two weeks away and technically I was still a student. Back to Amazon.

Amazon is indeed like a grocery store and so I could return the unwanted product. It would be a different case if I had read the book and decided to return it.

The Eighth Saturday

On the Confessions of a Humiliated Teacher

The Spring quarter finished quickly; I wanted to visit Father Schall and share with him about my spring quarter, but I did not have a chance to visit Los Gatos. Immediately after the exam week, I had to go to Chicago to attend two important Jesuits events. The first event was the Jesuit Conference – Association of Jesuit Colleges and Universities Meeting on Higher Education. The second event was the annual eight-day retreat for the first year Jesuit Regents in Bellarmine Retreat House in Barrington, Illinois.

After these two events, initially, I had a plan to go to San Diego for my summer program. The original plan was for me to work with the Indonesian Catholic Community in the area. The Matriarch of the community was from the same village where my dad grew up. She invited me to come and help the community with bible studies, spiritual conversation, etc. Nevertheless, during my retreat in Barrington, I experienced a health scare. It was on the fifth day of the retreat; I woke up at around 3 AM, went to the restroom, and noticed blood in my urine. I went to a nearby urgent care facility on the following morning and the doctor said that a urinary tract infection most likely caused it. I called my doctor in Santa Clara and made an appointment to see her upon my return home. My doctor immediately ordered a renal ultrasound test because she thought that urinary tract infections were very uncommon for males. Hence, she wanted to check whether there was a kidney stone or renal issue.

I decided to postpone my trip to San Diego until I received the results from my medical tests. Because of the postponement, now I had time to visit Father Schall in Los Gatos. I emailed Father Schall about my visit and said that I wanted to come earlier because there was something important that I wanted to discuss with him. On the first Saturday of July, I finally met Father Schall after almost two months. Per the regulation that a Jesuit can't receive a visitor in his room, Father Schall came to see me in the West Wing of the Infirmary. He asked me to walk outside and enjoy the beautiful summer day. But instead of going out the nearest door, we made a little detour through the infirmary. Father Schall said he would like to introduce me to some elderly Jesuits in the infirmary. Most of the infirm Jesuits were either sleeping or being cared by the nurse. So we did not have a chance to talk with many Jesuits.

The only Jesuit that we spent time with was a 98 year old priest named Father Carl Hayn. Father Hayn's lifetime ministry was in the physics classroom at Santa Clara University beginning in 1955. He taught full time for over 50 years, retiring in 2006 when partial hearing loss made classroom teaching more difficult. We stopped at Father Hayn's room and he looked good for a man who was almost 100 years old. Father Schall proudly introduced me as a Jesuit regent at Santa Clara University. We chatted for a few minutes, especially about life at Santa Clara University. I had heard about the legendary Father Hayn and so I had a few things to mention based on the intel that I received from the Jesuit community dining room. One of them was that it was Father Hayn's regular pastoral ministry was to celebrate 6:00 AM daily Mass in the Mission Church at the Guadalupe chapel.

Having spent a few minutes in Father Hayn's room, we moved out of his room and walked outside. "Tell me what happened," said Father Schall. I began with the story of my health scare during the retreat. Immediately after the retreat, I wrote an email to my Rector to inform him about my situation. When I opened my inbox, I found an email from the Dean of College of Art & Sciences of Santa Clara University, which informed me that the College has decided to reduce my teaching load from 2 courses to 1 course for the coming academic year. I would still be teaching one class at the Law School, but my primary working hours for the College of Art & Sciences had been shifted to advising instead of teaching. Indeed, I had had rough teaching experiences in the Winter and Spring quarters, but I thought it unfair to judge my teaching by those two quarters. The Dean simply made the decision based on the teaching evaluations and he never called me or heard my story. Moreover, the decision was a demotion and I didn't know why the Dean wanted to punish me for this humiliating experience. In his email, the Dean simply said that he believed I needed further supervision in teaching and so the second year would be a time for me to receive supervision. The Dean's message was somewhat strange to me because the College never provided any supervision in my first year of teaching, and later, the supervision was never given in my second year.

Father Schall first reaction was, "You should take care of your health. Your health is important. Remember that your health is important." I was a bit surprised to hear his first concern was my health instead of my teaching, emphasizing twice the importance of my health. He went on to say that I must treasure my health before I had to experience as many health scares as he had.

This statement made me think about my relationship with Father Schall. I had known him only for a brief period and so far, our conversations were mostly focused on some intellectual issues and a little bit about my life. I had not gotten a chance to learn about his life, especially about his health situation. For instance, I knew that Father Schall wore a regular pair of glasses, in which one lens was darkened. But I didn't know what happened to his left eye. I also notice that Father Schall had a problem with hypersalivation, in which extra saliva dripped out of his mouth continuously. Whenever I came to visit his room (before the no room visit policy), I always saw Father Schall tuck an extra-large napkin into his neck while he was working on his computer, which seemed like a remedy again the constant hypersalivation. But I didn't feel comfortable asking about his health history at that moment. Maybe one day I would know him well enough for him to share his health history with me. I resolved to pay more attention to his health, for while his mind was undeniably sharp, I knew little about his overall physical health.

I told Father Schall I would take his advice seriously and do my best to take care of myself. I told him I had been trying to create a more healthy lifestyle through exercise (primarily swimming) and a vegetarian diet. "Yeah, I can see that you always eat fruit and vegetables when we have a meal together," said Father Schall.

Father Schall then brought up the topic I most wanted to discuss with him – my apparent demotion. Surprisingly, he tried to assure me that it was not a demotion. He said, "You might see it as a demotion, but think about it, they assigned you more hours to advise students. If they didn't trust you anymore, they wouldn't give you the responsibility of advising students." I wasn't sure if Father Schall was trying to sugarcoat my situation, or if he was encouraging me, or maybe both. Deep in my heart, I believed that this decision was still unfair because demotions shouldn't be the price to pay for a struggling young professor like myself. Don't they know that teachers need time to learn their jobs properly?

Father Schall then asked if anything good came out of the student evaluations. I responded, "They gave me a high rating on my availability to help them outside the class."

"See? At least they appreciate your help outside the classroom. There is something special about you that the students might not see in other professors."

While it was true that they appreciated my availability outside the classroom, the overall evaluation was still bad. I feared this demotion would be a nail in the coffin of my teaching career at Santa Clara. I doubted I would have an opportunity to teach again at Santa Clara University in the future. Yet I hoped I might perhaps teach elsewhere after my ordination.

Father Schall stated further, "The problem is that you are new and so the students do not know you. If they know you, it will be easier to build trust." Father Schall explained that trust means that students will have confidence in the professor's knowledge of the subject matter. It also entailed the students' willingness to approach the professor when they had trouble understanding the subject.

Father Schall might have been correct in assuming that my students and I lacked a trusting relationship. They probably saw me as a young and inexperienced professor, an Asian man who spoke with a funny accent, and a Jesuit in training. On top of that, they saw me as someone who never experienced undergraduate study in the

United States, despite my Ph.D. from one of the top universities in the United States.

But Father Schall didn't stop encouraging me and sharing his wisdom. He noted that one of the problems of modern universities, where parents pay a considerable amount to keep their children in the classroom, was that the relationship between teacher and student is commonly perceived as a customer-seller relationship. Students consider themselves as customers because their parents have paid to send them to college. This encourages students to view their relationship with a professor as a business exchange between buyer and seller, in which the professor as the seller must provide the best service to the students as the customer or buyer.

"Yes, that is what I feel about some of my students at Santa Clara. Indeed, their parents must pay around $ 40,000 per year for their tuition. Then they think that they are entitled to a good grade."

"The teacher-student relationship is supposed to be spiritual and not contractual," said Father Schall.

I never heard about the notion of the spiritual relationship between teacher-student and asked Father Schall to explain it to me. Father explained that students are also spiritual beings with souls, and so the order of their souls must correspond to the order of reality. Being a teacher is being able to hand over to your students what you pondered and contemplated in your soul. Being a good teacher is not only to master a subject matter but to also have a soul that is free to see beyond itself.

A teacher is tasked with helping their students find order in their souls. First, a teacher must help the student to determine whether a non-arbitrary standard of free human behavior exists. For instance, the distinction between "what is right" and "what is wrong" is not something arbitrary. Second, once the student understands and establishes the standard, they must decide how to live up to those standards. Thus, it is never right to do wrong, and it is not right to justify wrongdoing.

"You still have a long journey to learn to be a good teacher, so don't feel discouraged by this experience. A student evaluation can sometimes be helpful, but it can also be vindictive or worthless, so don't pay too much attention to it," said Father Schall.

We stopped our conversation on that note; we had been walking around the Los Gatos compound for a little while and it was time for lunch. We had lunch with some elderly Jesuits and made small talk for the rest of the afternoon.

After lunch, I said goodbye to Father Schall, and he asked me to give him an update about my health if I heard something from the doctor about my lab test. I thanked him for his advice. When I got home, I tried to reflect on the wisdom he had shared with me. Indeed, he seemed a good father figure, a good source of encouragement. He did not judge me harshly, but tried to bring forth the best in me.

Summer in San Diego:

Standing on the Shoulders of Giants

On July 15, 2014, I went to see my doctor and she told me that the renal ultrasound test was negative. There were neither kidney stones nor renal issues, as she had previously feared. Nevertheless, she ordered me further testing to ensure there was nothing wrong with the rest of my body. The next test was a testicular ultrasound.

As my trip to San Diego was delayed, I asked permission from my doctor to postpone the medical test until early August, after my return from San Diego. I decided to shorten my stay in San Diego to three weeks instead of the whole summer. My doctor consented and finally cleared me to leave for San Diego. I drove from Santa Clara to San Diego. After stopping overnight in Los Angeles, I finally arrived in San Diego. The local superior at the Grape Street Jesuit Community assigned me the tiniest room in the house. In some ways, it reminded me of the cupboard under the stairs in the Harry Potter series - the small room where Harry Potter sleeps in Dursley's house, which contained only one bed. It turned out the tiny room was part of a larger room, which was considered the "penthouse" of the former Superior. When the new superior arrived a year before, in the spirit of the vow of poverty, he decided to cut the "penthouse" into a few smaller rooms.

The original plan was for me to serve the Indonesian Catholic Community in the area. But soon I realized that there was not much I could do because I was not a priest. Nevertheless, the community were happy to have me there. The activities with the Indonesian community took place mostly during the weekend. Consequently, I made myself busy during the weekdays. I decided to use my time to write a long article on the recent U.S. Supreme Court decision, *Hobby Lobby v. Burwell.* The point of departure of my essay was the work of Leo Strauss who argued that men need to choose between philosophy (Athens) or revelation (Jerusalem) as the ultimate answer to guide their lives. The tension between Jerusalem and Athens in *Hobby Lobby* could be found in two important issues: whether providing emergency contraception is a sinful act; and whether the state should commit itself to protect certain theistic beliefs or remain neutral. I argued that the Court majority opinion, written by Justice Samuel Alito, had taken the correct approach in *Hobby Lobby* by stating that it was not for the Court to say that the claimants' religious beliefs were mistaken or unreasonable. By respecting the sincerity of the claimants' religious beliefs, the Court committed itself to protecting religious truth.

I emailed Father Schall, letting him know that the doctor cleared me from any health scares, and I was currently in San Diego for my summer service. I wouldn't be able to visit him for the next few weeks. I promised to come to Los Gatos upon my return to Santa Clara. I told him about the article I was writing and asked if he could recommend further reading for my research on Leo Strauss. He wrote back to me and recommended the book by Susan Orr, *Jerusalem and Athens: Reason and Revelation in the Work of Leo Strauss.*

I had no choice other than working from my "cupboard" room. But sometimes I took a break by visiting the used bookstore. My favorite place was the iconic Adams Avenue Bookstore[14], a 10 minute drive from the Jesuit community where I stayed. I enjoyed my time in the used bookstore, never knowing what treasures I would find. Father Schall himself was a big fan of used bookstores. He believed that a visit to a used bookstore was both a humbling and exhilarating experience— "humbling to be reminded of how much you do not know, exhilarating to find there something that you would like to know and read."[15]

One of the highlights of my visits to the Adams Avenue bookstore was finding a book titled, *On the Intelligibility of Political Philosophy: Essays of Charles N.R. McCoy*, edited by Father James V. Schall. After I bought the book, I could not wait to get home and email Father Schall about my finding. But I read the book a little bit before I emailed Father Schall that evening. I had heard that Father McCoy was a mentor of Father Schall, but I was surprised to read in his biography that he was a professor at Santa Clara University. I emailed Father Schall and shared the story of finding the book. Also, I wondered why I never heard the name of Father McCoy among the Jesuits at Santa Clara University. I presumed that Father McCoy was a Jesuit priest because he mentored Father Schall and worked at a Jesuit institution.

---

[14] The Adam Avenue Bookstore closed down on July 14, 2018, after a 53-year run in San Diego.

[15] James V. Schall, *On the Push for Paperless and Revisiting Used Book Stores*, https://www.catholicworldreport.com/2014/10/06/on-the-push-for-paperless-and-revisiting-used-book-stores/

Father Schall wrote back to me and confirmed that Father McCoy indeed taught at Santa Clara University, but he was not a Jesuit priest; instead, he was ordained a diocesan priest in the Archdiocese of St. Paul, Minnesota. Father McCoy taught at the Catholic University of American for many years. He then moved to Santa Clara University as a Professor of Political Science and continued to live in Santa Clara until his death. Father Schall said that although Father McCoy was not generally well known among political theorists, it was worth reading his works. He recommended I dive into the book I found, and read the only book that Father McCoy wrote, *The Structure of Political Thought*. Father Schall explained that although Father McCoy's writings did not constitute a large corpus, they were very rich in the nature and meaning of political philosophy.

I began to read the collection of Father McCoy's essays, and I found two important take-aways from reading the book. First, Father McCoy followed the constitutional law side of political science and combined it with classical theory. In his article on the *Doctrine of Judicial Review and Natural Law*, Father McCoy began with a classical analysis on the theory of natural law, relying on Aristotle and Thomas Aquinas. He then argued in the beginning that judicial review was related to the natural law, in which he analyzed the U.S. Supreme Court decision in *Marbury v. Madison*. Justice Marshall approached the case by asking three different questions. The first question was whether the applicant (Marbury) had a right to the commission. The second question was if he had a right and had that right been violated, did the laws afford him a remedy? The third question was if the laws did afford Marbury a remedy, was this remedy a mandamus issued from the Supreme Court.

Father McCoy argued that in answering the first and second questions, the Court's conclusion was based on the principle of natural law instead of federal statute. To the first question, the Court held that Marbury's appointment was made when the President signed a commission. The commission was complete when the Secretary of State affixed the seal of the United States to it. Therefore, withholding the commission was "an act deemed by the Court not warranted by law, but violative of a vested legal right." Similarly, the answer to the second question, Chief Justice Marshal observed that "the government of the United States has been emphatically termed a government of laws, and not of men. It will certainly cease to deserve this high appellation if the laws furnish no remedy for the violation of a vested legal right." Here Father McCoy argued that what Chief Justice Marshall was saying was that the laws must provide such a remedy whether there was a specific statutory provision or not.

For the last question, however, the Court used a legal analysis on the distinction between the Supreme Court's original and appellate jurisdiction. The original jurisdiction in the Constitution was already final and Congress had no power to add to that jurisdiction. The Court did not find, among the items listed in the Constitution, an authority to issue the writ of mandamus within its jurisdiction. Therefore, the Court held it lacked original jurisdiction to issue a writ of mandamus.

My second take away was that there was a profoundly Thomistic spirit in the works of Father McCoy. Nevertheless, his works did not flow from any slavish following of St. Thomas, but from a careful analysis of the divergent positions taken in the history of political philosophy in the light of the analysis of Aristotle and St. Thomas. For instance, in his essay *The Meaning of Jean-Jacques Rousseau and the Structure of Political Theory*, Father McCoy observed that the whole of eighteenth-century thought was based on the understanding that "the autonomy of the intellect corresponds to the pure autonomy of nature."[16] To refute this postulate, Father McCoy referred to the Greek-Medieval tradition in philosophy, the pure autonomy of nature was not simply corresponding with the autonomy of intellect. He referred to Aristotle's *Physics*, which demonstrates that nature acts for an end, but it is not directed by rational principle intrinsic to itself. In his commentary on the *Physics*, St. Thomas defines nature as a "reason put in things by the Divine art so that they can act for an end."[17] For both Aristotle and St. Thomas, nothing is done in nature without the cooperation of the divine.[18] In sum, the

---

[16] Charles McCoy, "The Meaning of Jean-Jacques Rousseau in Political Theory," in James V. Schall and John J. Schrems (eds), *On the Intelligibility of Political Philosophy: Essays of Charles N. R. McCoy* (Washington DC: The Catholic University of American Press, 1989), 66.

[17] St. Thomas Aquinas, *Commentaria in octo libros Physicorum*, lib. 2 l. 14 n. 8, Corpus Thomiscum, https://www.corpusthomisti-cum.org/cpy012.html: *Unde patet quod natura nihil est aliud quam ratio cuiusdam artis, scilicet divinae, indita rebus, qua ipsae res moventur ad finem determinatum: sicut si artifex factor navis posset lignis tribuere, quod ex se ipsis moverentur ad navis formam inducendam.*

[18] St. Thomas Aquinas, *Summa Contra Gentiles* III, 65: *nulla igitur res remanere potest in esse, cessante operatione divina.*

ends of human life do not depend on our simple will, but it depends on the will of God, as the things of art depend on the will of the artist.

I emailed Father Schall and shared my observations about Father McCoy's thought. Father Schall wrote to me and explained several things about his mentor. First, Father McCoy earned his doctorate in political science on constitutional law at the University Chicago before his ordination as a priest. He did not get a political philosophy degree at Chicago because Charles E. Merriam, who is generally recognized as the founder and shaper of the Chicago School of Political Science, would only consider a certain view of politics. Charles Merriam was instrumental in pushing away the Political Science from European-style theoretical discussion into actual research, with data and quantitative analysis in the practice of political science. Moreover, Merriam was the leading thinker of the political philosophy of progressivism, as manifested in his notable book *A History of American Political Theories*. Merriam preferred a different form of political theory to classical-medieval political theory. Thus, by writing a dissertation on constitutional law, McCoy was avoiding Merriam's progressive political philosophy. After his ordination, McCoy did his second doctoral studies in Laval University, Quebec and studied under the auspices of Charles de Koninck, where he perfected his studies in St. Thomas.

Father Schall explained further that Father McCoy was already considered "ancient history" in his time due to his fondness of Aquinas. The Catholic circles had already abandoned Aquinas during McCoy's time. One of the reasons for the abandonment of Aquinas among priests in general and priest scholars in particular was due to poor teaching in seminaries. Thus, McCoy's works in retrospect

were significant because he showed that the small error in the beginning, the abandonment of Thomism, would eventually lead to large
errors in the end.

On that evening, in my "cupboard" room in San Diego, I reflected on the lives of Father McCoy and Father Schall. I remember
that a few years ago, George Weigel praised Father Schall as part of
the generation of giants that emerged from the Catholic intellectual
renaissance of the mid-20th century.[19] Weigel posited that the most
urgent question facing Catholic higher education today was how Catholicism "[received] great priests and teachers like Father Schall" as
luminaries of that generation passed from the scene. Father McCoy
was in some way part of the generation of giants, although he was
considered one generation before Father Schall.

I began to ponder whether or not my generation would be able
to carry that much-needed torch. I once shared my thoughts about
this with a newly ordained Jesuit priest and he rather cynically replied that my generation should not have any illusions about being
able to fill the shoes of those giants. He believed that we didn't have
the conditions that formed the intellectual greats of the past, such as
a common intellectual patrimony rooted in the tradition of the West
and well-established schools of philosophy and theology.

Perhaps he was correct to think we will never see the emergence
of such a generation again. But I have hope that my generation can
carry the torch. I have confidence that by following the prescription

---

[19] George Weigel, George. "In Praise of Father Schall. *First Things*, July
28, 2010. https://www.firstthings.com/web-exclusives/2010/07/in-praise-
of-father-schall

from Sertillanges' *Intellectual Life*, I can build a solid foundation in the intellectual life. But for now, I needed to finish my article on *Hobby Lobby in between Athens and Jerusalem*.

The Ninth Saturday

A Doctor Who Does Not Care about a Patient's Soul

I left San Diego in early August and returned to Santa Clara. I immediately conducted the testicular ultrasound test as prescribed by my doctor. While I was waiting for the lab test result, a fellow Jesuit, Kevin Embach contacted me and said that he was planning to stop by Santa Clara University to visit me in the final leg of a road trip to California. Moreover, he wanted me to arrange a meeting with Father Schall, whom he considered his favorite author.

I planned to visit Father Schall anyway, so I emailed him and said that I was planning to visit him with a fellow Jesuit from the Midwest Province. Father Schall said he was happy to welcome us and was looking forward to seeing us that Saturday morning. Kevin Embach is a compassionate man, but he is infamous for his chaotic schedule. He arrived on Friday evening at Santa Clara after a long drive from Los Angeles and planned to leave on the following day, around early afternoon, from San Francisco airport (SFO). Considering that a drive from Santa Clara to SFO was at least 40 minutes and Kevin had to be in the airport two hours earlier, we only had a tiny window to see Father Schall. Our only option was to see Father Schall in the morning instead of lunch time. I did not bother to email Father Schall because I thought he knew that we were coming, and he would be around Los Gatos anyway.

On the following morning, we drove to Los Gatos and arrived there around 9 AM. But when the nurse in the infirmary station called Father Schall's room, he was not there. The nurse tried to find him but Father Schall was nowhere to be found. Finally, the nurse called the local Superior, Father John Privett, S,J and tried to find Father Schall's whereabout. Father Privett came to see us and explained that Father Schall was taking "Conversations That Matter," the continuing education program for Jesuits of the United States on creating safe environments for children and vulnerable adults. After the wave of the sexual abuse scandal in the United States, the Society of Jesus implemented policies and procedures for protecting children and vulnerable adults. The policies are accredited by Praesidium, Inc, which provides training materials for preventing sexual misconduct. Every Jesuit in the United States must participate in this Praesidium Training, including an eighty-six-year-old Jesuit like Father Schall.

Father Privett explained to us that the rest of Jesuits had taken the training a few months ago, but Father Schall did not participate in Conversations That Matter because he was travelling out of town. So that morning was the last opportunity for Father Schall to take the Praesidium training. We knew that the training would last around two hours and Kevin Embach could not wait that long because he had to catch his flight back to Chicago. So, we left a message for Father Schall that we had visited but were unable to see him. Before we left the premises, I asked Father Privett about the policy of visitors not spending time in the Jesuit's private room. I understood that there was a boundary issue between the Jesuits and lay visitors, but I wondered if there was an exception for a Jesuit Scholastic like myself so that I could visit Father Schall in his room instead of having him come down to see me. Father Privett simply said, "Tell the nurse that you are a Jesuit and you have obtained a permission from me to visit Jim in his room." I thanked Father Privett.

We went back to Santa Clara and Kevin Embach left immediately in his rental car for the San Francisco airport. When I got back to my room and checked the email, I saw Father Schall's email in my mailbox. First, he apologized for missing us that morning and he told me to come back to visit him at any time when I was available. It was little after 11 AM and I still had time to return to Los Gatos for lunch with Father Schall. So, I wrote back to Father Schall and told him I was coming back to Los Gatos to see him.

I arrived in Los Gatos right before lunch, so Father Schall and I immediately sat down to lunch. Again, Father Schall apologized for the situation that morning and said that he would write a personal email to Kevin Embach and apologize for missing him. I thought about this kind of humility from an elderly priest like Father Schall who wanted to apologize personally to a Jesuit Scholastic like Kevin Embach. Father Schall then asked me to tell him a little bit about Kevin. I told him that Kevin was a native of Detroit, he went to the undergraduate program at the University of Notre Dame and then went to medical school at the University of Virginia. Having spent twenty years in medical practice, he decided to enter the Jesuit Novitiate. His favorite book was Father Schall's *The Order of Things*.

"I am surprised to hear that he loves that book as a medical doctor because I was critical to his profession in the first chapter of the book," said Father Schall. In the chapter, "The Orderly and the Divine," Father Schall told a story of how, when he was in a hospital waiting room for an examination, he was asked to sign a waiver. Father Schall said that the wavier form was an indication that the hospital and doctors know that the medicine was not an exact science and things might go wrong. Father Schall argued that the waiver was also a sign that a doctor only cares about bodily health but is not concerned with his patient's soul or the ultimate purpose of his patient's life. To discover the ultimate purpose and the state of his soul, Father Schall argued that he would have to go somewhere else instead of to a doctor.

"Maybe your friend is a humble doctor who admits the flaws in the medical profession," Father Schall guessed about Kevin Embach.

"Kevin Embach is indeed a humble man, but he has a tremendous pride for his profession, so I don't think that he would agree with your opinion."

"I wonder why he still considers my book as his favorite book."

"I have an explanation, but I won't say it here."

Since we already discuss a hospital and doctors, I decided to use this opportunity to ask Father Schall about his health history. I asked, "Father Schall, the story of your visit to the doctor in the book, was that related to your eyes, if I may ask?"

"No, I lost my left eye in the summer of 1989 when I had torn my retina. After the fifth surgery failed, I knew that I would not see out of my left eye again."

Father Schall continued, "I wrote that book around 2005, long after I lost my eye. I had so many surgeries and hospital visits, so it's hard to keep track of which visit I referred to in that book. So, treasure your health while you can."

Father Schall then asked me about the latest update of my health. I felt a bit embarrassed because it was Father Schall who asked me about my health instead of me asking him about his health. I told Father Schall that I was still waiting for the lab test results from the testicular ultrasound, and I hoped that this would be the last test and that I wouldn't need to see a specialist. Father Schall then made a joke about how you know the truth about your age when your address book contains many names ending in MD.

"Well, at one point in my life, I had a special doctor who was on my speed dial," I told Father Schall.

"Were you sick or under special treatment?"

"No, she was my fiancée."

"You broke with her and joined the Novitiate?"

"No, it's a long story."

I began to tell my story of my ex-fiancée, Linda. It all started during the heyday of the student movement in Indonesia. When some leaders of the student movement were arrested, there was an Indonesian Jesuit priest who helped them through the prison ministry. The then Jesuit priest ran a group under the banner of the Volunteer Team for Humanity. He recruited some young students, including some female medical students from a Catholic University in Jakarta. One of the volunteers, Catherine, developed a romantic relationship with one of the student leaders, Budiman Sudjatmiko. To make a long story short, Catherine had a good friend from medical school named Linda. Catherine then arranged with her boyfriend to introduce Linda to me.

In retrospect, I often wonder why those female medical students wanted to start a romantic relationship with crazy activists like us. Of course, love is always a mystery, but I think one of the plausible explanations was that they saw us as heroes who brought down the military regime. After I started my relationship with Linda, she invited me to come to Mass with her. At that time, I had been away from the Catholic Church for almost five years. I decided to attend Sunday Mass simply because I wanted to please her. Having spent many months attending Mass with Linda, the Gospel message slowly began to penetrate my heart; I started to re-examine my life, and finally made my first confession in five years.

To cut the story short, we had been dating for six years when I decided to pursue my graduate studies. At that time, Linda had been practicing medicine for a little while and she said that she did not want to wait for me for another five years until I finished my Ph.D. She gave me an ultimatum, "marry me now or never." I was torn because deep in my heart I knew that I was not ready to get married, but I did not want to lose her either. So, I tried to please her; we planned to marry after my first year in Seattle. The wedding date was set for August 21, 2005; the chapel and the wedding reception were booked, including the catering company. Before I left the country for my graduate studies, Linda pushed me to pay the down payment for those venues, which I did.

My first year in the US was rough because of the academic pressure and a new life in a new country. At the same time, I had been praying a lot to God and asked his guidance and clarity on what I should do about my wedding plans. I knew that deep in my heart, I was not ready to be a husband and a father, but I didn't know what to do because we already engaged. On top of that, I was not sure if I would be happy in my married life with Linda. I loved her but we had engaged in many conflicts over the years. Consequently, we had

been torturing each other in our relationship. Some of those conflicts arose out petty issues - Linda was a hygiene freak and so we
fought a lot about cleanliness and hygiene.

I had been praying for months and God did not seem to answer
my prayers. I didn't know what to do about my marriage plan.
Around the same time, I met a social anthropologist from Cornell
University named Dee (not her real name), who was doing her research on the student movement in Indonesia. We met for the first
time in Jakarta and remained in contact after I left for the United
States. In some ways, I felt more compatible with Dee because she
cared less about hygiene and germs. I thought that maybe this was
God's answer to my prayer. But I knew that I must have the courage
to end my relationship with Linda first before I made an overture to
Dee. In April 2005, after seven years of dating and less than four
months before our wedding, I told Linda that it would be better for
us to end our relationship and cancel our wedding. After the end of
my drama with Linda, I approached Dee with the idea of dating, but
she simply said, "I enjoyed our intellectual exchange, but no more
no less." So, I ended up with nothing that summer.

Having listened to my story, Father Schall said, "Your life story
is like a movie and someday it should be made into a movie."

"I don't think there will be any producers who are interested in
my story."

"Well, you never know. What happened after that?"

"It's still a long story, but in retrospect, Linda was a doctor who
cared about my soul. She was the one who helped me to get back to
my faith. Maybe it was not her intention, but God worked through
her."

"I guess that you are the only patient whose soul she cared about!"

We both laughed and ended our lunch on that note. I promised Father Schall I would share the rest of my story on my next visit. I remembered that I still owed him the story of my conversion and it all related to the account of my post-relationship with Linda. I said goodbye to Father Schall and told him that I hoped to visit him soon.

The Tenth Saturday

On Natural Law, Abortion, and Tiger Moms

In early September, I came back to Los Gatos to visit Father Schall. I arrived earlier that Saturday because I wanted to discuss my independent study class on Natural Law with him. There was a student who was interested in doing an independent study on Natural Law, and I was happy to help her. I had emailed Father Schall and asked his recommendations on reading materials that I could use for the class. I used some of Father Schall's reading recommendations and combined it with some of my personal reading list.

Upon my arrival in Los Gatos, Father Schall invited me to walk outside and enjoy the late summer weather. We walked toward the Grotto of the Blessed Mother and Father Schall asked me to sit with him on the bench near the Grotto. We were facing the valley, with the Grotto behind us. I told Father Schall that my independent study class had just begun and currently my student was reading a book that he recommended, titled *Natural Law: An Introduction To Legal Philosophy* by the Italian philosopher, Alessandro Passerin d'Entrèves. I pulled the slender book from my backpack and showed it to Father Schall. I had bought the used book online via Amazon.com, but it was still in good condition. Father Schall opened the book and looked at the inscription on the front page. "What is written here?" After trying to guess what was written, Father Schall said, "I thought my handwriting is the most illegible but there is someone else who probably has worse handwriting than mine." Indeed, the handwriting of the previous owner of the book was illegible. The only words that I could read were "Michigan, 1959."

"Did your student like reading this book?" asked Father Schall.

"I think that she is doing okay, but the problem is she often has difficulty understanding the concept. Maybe it is because she has no solid background in philosophy."

"It's common that students who are just learning about Natural Law do not understand the concepts in the first reading. But ask her to reread it, two or three times. My students usually have a better understanding after reading it several times."

"It's a good idea; I will ask her to reread it several times."

"Even if she has difficulty understanding the concept now, it's fine. Understanding Natural Law is not an instant process. She might not understand it now, but she might able to put the pieces of the puzzle together in the future if she keeps reading and learning about it."

Father Schall was right in his thoughts about learning and reading natural law. I took a class on natural in my first semester at philosophy study. But it took a while for the concepts to sink in my head. As I keep reading and learning about the ideas throughout the years, I slowly put together the pieces and understood it gradually.

Father Schall tried to translate the handwriting in the book one more time, but he gave up and gave the book back to me, saying, "My mother always said that the purpose of letters is to be read and she waged an unsuccessful campaign for years to have me type my letters. Maybe the mother of the previous owner of this book also said the same thing to her son."

Father Schall then asked me, "Do you talk or write to your mother often?"

"Yes, I talk to her quite often over the phone."

"It's good to hear that you have a good relationship with your mother. It can be a nightmare if you don't have a good relationship with your mom after your dad rejects you."

"Well, my relationship with my mom is not great either."

I had a complicated relationship with my mom, who imposed a strict parenting style upon me. A few years ago, the infamous tiger mom, Amy Chua, published her parenting memoir, *Battle Hymn of the Tiger Mother*, in which she told of her strict parenting towards her daughters.[20] When I read the book, it reminded me of my childhood because I was also a "tiger cub." I remember that when I was in the fourth grade, I had a C in my math class and my mom made me do math problems for four to five hours a night and did not let me have a bathroom break until I got it right.

Also, I did not have a good relationship with mom because of my little sister. When I was a little boy, my mom demanded I protect and oversee my sister in school. This felt like a tremendous burden to me because I was unable to defend even myself from the bullies in school, so how could I protect my little sister? Often, my mom blamed me for my failure to protect my sister and called me a "useless brother." When my sister began her application to the Middle School, my mom immediately asked me to prepare the application for my sister and even requested that I accompany my sister to the

---

[20] Amy Chua, *The Battle Hymn of the Tiger Mother*, (New York: The Penguin Press, 2011).

interview. When the School accepted my sister's application, I had to meet the Principal and deal with all the administrative work. I still remember vividly: the Principal joking that I was too young to have a daughter who was about to attend middle school. Indeed, I was too young to be a parent, but my mom made me a "parentified child."

When I became a teenager, I began to turn against my mother's strict parenting and challenged her. When my mom wanted to choose my major in college, I lied to her, telling her I would comply, but instead choosing a different major against her wishes. Upon my graduation from college, I began to maintain total independence from my parents. Since then I always reminded myself that I am an independent man and I don't need anyone. The bottom line was that I didn't want to be controlled or bothered by anyone.

Considering my mother was a tiger mom, I always wanted to find a better mother figure. Therefore, I easily turned toward the Holy Mary Mother of God. In the Blessed Mother, I found a better mother. In my prayer's life, I developed a special devotion to the Blessed Mother, as she is a gentle, caring, and loving mother. This I pondered, as I sat then in the shadow of the Grotto of the Blessed Mother.

"The fact that you still speak with her frequently signifies that you still have a decent relationship with your mom," said Father Schall. He continued, "If your mom also rejected you like your dad did, then it would really kill you and you wouldn't be the person you are today. Don't you think you benefitted from her strict parenting? It's hard to be a confident man without your dad's encouragement, but it seems that you still had a mother who helped you to be a courageous man."

I admitted, however begrudgingly, that the discipline my mother imposed upon me probably made me a more organized and confident adult.

Knowing that the subject of my mom is not easy, Father Schall switched the topic of conversation by asking me, "How is everything in Santa Clara?"

"The latest is news is that Santa Clara University is going to pay for abortions after the State of California ruled that they can't refuse to cover the cost of abortions."

When I arrived at Santa Clara University in Fall of 2013, the University notified employees that they would stop paying for elective abortions. But the majority of the University employees objected to the decision. Those disgruntled faculties then formed an alliance with Planned Parenthood and the ACLU to lobby the women's caucus of the California Legislature, which in turn asked Governor Jerry Brown to clarify that even religious nonprofits must cover abortion in their employee benefit plans. Brown's administration then ruled that Santa Clara University and other Catholic universities must offer abortion coverage in their health insurance plans.

"That is very pathetic... why they didn't fight the decision? What's the point of having a Law School if you can't defend yourselves?" said Father Schall.

"Well, the problem is that most of the law school faculty are proponents of abortion rights, so they are happy with Jerry Brown's decision."

Father Schall just smiled to hear my answer and continued, "I am sure those people tend to be horrified by the number of deaths in Nazi, Soviet, and Muslim worlds, but it's strange that they are not horrified by abortions statistics, which reveal to us that we kill on a much larger scale than those movements. Do you know the number of abortions in the world since 1980?"

"I am not sure, maybe 500 million?"

Father Schall raised his voice, "1.5 billion."

"I know that abortion in the U.S. since *Roe v. Wade* was around 60 million, but I didn't know the worldwide abortion statistics were that high."

"The conflicting views about abortion statistics and deaths because of war is an interesting topic for your natural law class. You should discuss it with your students."

"Yes, I am already scheduling a session to discuss natural law and abortion. I am planning to discuss a book by Hadley Arkes, *Natural Right and Right to Choose.*"

"Good. Hadley Arkes is a good friend of mine."

Father Schall then explained further that the justification for abortion could be traced back to the systematic rejection of natural law and natural reason in modern times. According to the natural law, there is an objective order; men discover moral law, but do not make the law. If men follow this natural order, they would be upholding all human life. But the rejection of this order leads step by step, gradually moving from normal sexual relations to the killing of a baby. Then the modern man believes that he is free from the judgment of the natural order and so refuses to consult anything in nature to determine what is right and what is wrong.

We finished our conversation on natural law and abortion; we left the Grotto and moved back to the house for lunch. After lunch, Father Schall walked with me to my car. Before I left, he asked me,

"By the way, how is your health situation? Any updates from the doctor?" I told Father Schall that my doctor recommended I see a urologist to discuss the results of the testicular ultrasound, which showed that I had a varicocele. The urologist said that varicoceles are very common; 15% of all adult men have them. More importantly, they are not dangerous. But varicoceles can cause impaired fertility. The doctor said that I needed to undergo surgery if I wanted to have a family because it might affect testosterone production. But I explained that I was a celibate man who had no desire to have a family. So, we agreed not to do surgery.

"Glad to hear that there is nothing serious and that thing is not dangerous," said Father Schall.

I said goodbye to Father Schall, thanked him for his time, and said that I hoped to come visit him again soon. "Please come at any time," he replied.

The Eleventh Saturday

Autumn Came Back to D.C.

The teaching obligations and work in campus ministry had delayed my visit to Father Schall. In early October, I emailed Father Schall about my plan to visit him on the following Saturday. But Father Schall replied that he wouldn't be around because he would be in D.C. that weekend. So I waited for another week. It was already the third Saturday of October when I finally had a chance to visit Los Gatos.

After checking in at the nurse station, I went to Father Schall's room and knocked on his door. "Come in," he said. I opened the door, and as usual, Father Schall was working on his computer. He invited me to sit down, and we started our conversation. I asked him how he was doing after his trip to D.C. He seemed fine other than being tired after taking such a long trip. I then asked him what he did in D.C. It turned out that he was attending the Annual Meeting of the American Catholic Philosophical Association.

"What was the topic of the talk or paper you delivered in the Conference?" I asked.

"It was about 'habits without metaphysics.'"

Honestly, "habits without metaphysics" was a foreign concept to me, so I asked for Father Schall's explanation.

Father Schall was referring to a French philosopher, Étienne Gilson, who argued that Augustinian metaphysics consists of realism, which includes body and soul. When he was young, Augustine had many bad habits and vices, and he tried to justify them with the theories of the Manicheans. The more mature Augustine finally realized that he could not simply find justification for his bad habits because to justify his sinful ways, he must construct a mental world deviant from the truth. He found truth in God's search for him, so the complete story was not just of Augustine pursuing the truth, but of God pursuing him.

Father Schall explained further that Augustine began, not with things beyond us, but with the restlessness in our souls. It means that no one is exempt from divine pursuit; either one is a great sinner or an ordinary person. But Augustine believed that most people do resist the divine pursuit. The possibility of resisting the divine searching is what Father Schall called "habits without metaphysics." Human beings form their habits by how they live and choose; they build a false picture of the world system to justify their preference. Their habits will then protect them from ever being aware of God's search for their immortal souls.

I told Father Schall that while I had no knowledge of the concept of habits without metaphysics, I could relate to the idea from my personal experience. It related to my conversion story, which I still needed to tell Father Schall. I took this opportunity to complete the story, as I promised a few months ago.

My first moment of conversion came a few years after my relationship with my then-girlfriend, Linda. To refresh the story, after the fall of the military regime, I emerged like a soldier who won the war. Apart from my arrogance as a student activist who was involved in bringing down the dictatorship, I had become an angry young man. Yet despite my ego, I was at an all-time low. My relationship with Linda fell apart because she could not stand me any longer. I barely had a friend outside the student movement. My relationship with my parents and my sister had been deteriorating for years because of my decision to distance myself from them. Moreover, I was being kicked out of the student movement due to an internal struggle in the movement. I was miserable, but at least I realized how depressed I was.

I didn't know what to do with myself. No one was around to talk to and with nowhere to go, in that moment of desperation, I turned to the Blessed Mother Mary. I knelt down and began to pray, "Mother Mary, I can't do this anymore. I need your help." I began to pray the rosary for the first time after many years, and I slowly grew in my devotion to the Blessed Mother. Things began to improve after this; I reconciled with Linda and rekindled our romantic relationship. At the same time, I slowly abandoned my political activism. Then I got a new job at an international law firm in Jakarta.

But it took a while for me to really come back to God and Holy Mother Church. I turned to Jesus via His Mother in that moment of desperation because I realized that I could not rely on my power alone. I needed to rely on the Divine's power. But I still had some reservations towards the institutional Church. Moreover, I had no sense of worshipping God with adoration, repentance, and thanksgiving.

Fast forward to my time in Seattle; I had a profound conversion experience. I ended my engagement with Linda and canceled the wedding. Then my overture towards Dee ended badly. As crushed as I was, I decided to move on and rebuild my life. In summer 2005,

I joined a camping trip with the young adults at the Catholic Newman Center. To be honest, my decision to become more involved in the Newman Center was motivated by my desire to meet like-minded women. On the camping trip, I met a young Indonesian lady who invited me to monthly Mass in the Indonesian language at the University of Washington Newman Center. I attended the Indonesian Mass with the primary motivation of getting to know the young Indonesian ladies in the group.

In November 2005, I joined a weekend retreat organized by the Indonesian Catholic Young Adult Group. The retreat took place at the Sambica Retreat Center, a non-denominational Christian retreat camp on the shores of Lake Sammamish, around 20 minutes east of Seattle. Again, my primary motivation was to get to know a young Indonesian lady from that group. But the retreat turned out to be a different experience for me. The facilitator of the retreat was an Indonesian Carmelite priest. On the second day of the retreat, all the participants had to maintain complete silence between lunch and dinner. We could walk or wander around the retreat camp, but all must be in silence. I decided to take a nap and stayed in my room. But I felt restless and could not close my eyes. In that moment of silence, I looked over my life and reflected that God had given me a good life. In retrospect, my family was poor, but we never lived in hunger or without shelter. Though the son of a poor miner, I had been blessed with an opportunity to enjoy a good education. I realized that I was angry with God because I felt that no one loved me; I did not feel the love of my parents, although they would say that they loved me. Projecting from that feeling came the feeling that God did not love me. But in that moment, I realized that God loved me, as demonstrated by the blessings he had poured on my life.

After dinner, we had an evening reflection. At this moment, I had an opportunity to reflect on the words of Jesus from John 15:15, "I have called you friends." Listening to these words, I realized that Jesus was indeed my loyal friend. In my lifetime, I hadn't had many friends because it was hard for me to build trust, as many people that I considered friends betrayed me. But I forgot that Jesus was also my loyal friend, and he remained loyal to me despite the fact that I had abandoned him.

Later, the Carmelite priests had a session on the outpouring of the Holy Spirit. I had no clue what it was about and was little bit skeptical, but at least I was open to it. The priest prayed over each of the retreatants. When he prayed over me, I felt the power of the Holy Spirit envelope me in what seemed like waves of electricity. I can only describe the experience as God's love and His power washing over me. I did not speak in tongues like other retreatants, but I could feel that I was shaking and fell on the ground. I felt that I was truly transformed that night.

On the following morning, I woke up a new person. I felt that the world was so beautiful with the shining sun, singing birds, and fresh air. It was Sunday morning, and we had a closing Mass before our departure. The Gospel reading at the Mass was Matthew 25, the parable of ten virgins who took their lamps and went out to meet the bridegroom. But the priest was preaching about the call to the priesthood and religious life. I found that his sermon was strange because it had no relation whatsoever to the Gospel. I had no desire to be a priest at that time; nevertheless, his message stuck with me. So in the end, instead of me pursuing that young lady, God was pursuing me in that retreat.

"It's amazing how God really works to pursue you. More importantly, you did not resist His pursuit. Someday you must write a book about your conversion like Augustine did," said Father Schall.

"Well, I don't think I can write a deep theological treatise like the *Confession*, but I can try to write something lighter."

"The *Confession* is pretty much a spiritual autobiography, with a little meditation and scriptural exegesis. You don't have to write something exactly like Augustine, but your story is important to be told and shared with many." Father Schall stopped for a moment and continued, "What time is it now?"

"It's around a quarter past noon."

"Let's go for lunch."

While we were walking to the dining room, I asked Father Schall, "Anything interesting from the Conference?"

"I met many good Catholic young men and women who have Ph.D.s in philosophy, but they could not find jobs at any Catholic universities. It's sad to hear their stories. They could not find jobs either because those universities do not teach philosophy any longer, or they don't want to hire faithful Catholic philosophers."

"What are those people doing now? Are they still teaching?"

"Some of them teach at small liberal arts colleges or even Protestant colleges, and some are independent scholars. When the time comes for you to find a job, you will be better prepared to deal with a similar reality. You might have to apply to non-Jesuit schools."

"It's still many years to go before my ordination, and right now, I just want to make sure I can survive this regency assignment."

We joined some other retired Jesuits for lunch, and the conversation was centered around Father's Schall's recent trip to D.C. They asked Father Schall how he felt returning to Washington, D.C. for the first time since his retirement. Father Schall said that he felt good because fall was the perfect time to visit D.C. with the combination of pleasant weather and beautiful foliage. Moreover, the conference took place in the Hyatt Regency at Capitol Hill, and the fall was the perfect time to wander around D.C. because there were less tourists in town. I asked Father Schall if he stayed in Georgetown and whether he missed Georgetown. Father Schall answered that he did stay in Georgetown and he missed it a bit. Still, he knew that his home was now in Los Gatos. Another Jesuit asked Father Schall whether he had a chance to greet Jack the Bulldog, the official university mascot. Father Schall explained that Jack Sr. (the nickname of the mascot), which was around during his time at Georgetown, had retired. But Jack Sr. continued to live on campus, spending his days resting in the lobby of the Jesuit Residence. Jack Jr. (known as J.J.) came in spring 2012, but the mascot duty did not work well for him, and he entered early retirement. So, the University President established a committee to determine how to continue the tradition. Then the committee brought a new bulldog from San Diego in Fall 2013. One of the Jesuits on our table asked, "The President brought the bulldog with him from San Diego?" Father Schall just smiled and explained that the President just formed a committee to find the new living mascot.

Another Jesuit then asked Father Schall, "Who is taking care of the dog, just anyone who is walking with him?"

Father Schall explained that there was a group of students who were responsible for walking the bulldog during the day and evening and escorting him to various events on campus. "Many guys like to walk the dog. Do you know why? Girls love guys with a dog. By walking the dog, those guys can interact with the girls."

It was indeed an interesting lunch conversation. It was funny to listen to these elderly, retired Jesuits busy talking about Jack the bulldog. But it was a good break from my serious conversation with Father Schall earlier that day. We finished lunch, and as usual, Father Schall walked with me to my car. I said goodbye and said that I hoped to see him again in the coming weeks.

The Twelfth Saturday

Lunch at a Chinese Restaurant

The end of October was a busy time for me with mid-terms and other obligations so I did not have a chance to visit Father Schall during that time. November came; I had to travel to Chicago for the Constitutional Law Colloquium at Loyola University Law School in the first weekend of November. I finally finished my paper on *Hobby Lobby in between Athens and Jerusalem*, and I was to present that paper in the colloquium. The conference in Chicago was fruitful but tiring. As I was recovering from the trip, I emailed Father Schall to let him know that I planned to see him the weekend before Thanksgiving. He emailed me back, saying that he would be around, but that the kitchen and dining room in Sacred Heart Jesuit Center were under construction, so there was no place to eat lunch. Father Schall told me further that he would be away for Thanksgiving break with his niece and wouldn't be back until early December. So I must wait until December to visit him.

I already had travel arrangements in early December for a Comparative Constitutional Law roundtable at my alma mater, University of Washington School of Law. After Seattle, I was leaving for Sydney, Australia to attend another conference, and then spending Christmas in Indonesia. In that case, I wouldn't have time to see him until after New Year, so I asked Father Schall if there was any chance that we could meet without lunch, if we could instead take a short walk or the like. Father Schall then proposed for us to have lunch outside, to which I willingly agreed.

Law School classes would be pretty much over before Thanksgiving, with the students just returning for final exams. I needed to prepare the examination questions before Thanksgiving. I was busy writing my exam questions when I realized it was almost time for my lunch appointment with Father Schall. I had just enough time to get to Los Gatos. However, when I went to get the car keys, I realized it had been already checked out by a fellow Jesuit. As Jesuits, we only have a communal car to be shared, and during the weekend, the car was much in use. I'd failed to sign out the car earlier and realized I might be unable to leave. Fortunately, there was a big van that we usually used for transporting stuff or people. I borrowed the van and drove to Los Gatos.

I arrived at Los Gatos a few minutes past noon, and Father Schall was already walking around the front yard of Sacred Heart Center, waiting for me. I apologized for coming a little late, explaining the van and how the car had been checked out. "You drive what you get, "said Father Schall with a smile. Father Schall got into the van, and I asked him where we would go. He proposed for us to have lunch at a Chinese restaurant, to which I immediately said yes. I marveled at Father Schall's memory for directions, as he guided me to the restaurant without any confusion.

We ordered some food and soft drinks, then Father Schall asked the Chinese lady who was serving us for two small straws. After his jaw surgery, Father Schall was not able to drink water from a glass or cup, so he needed a straw to drink. I already notice Father Schall's situation during my interactions with him in Los Gatos, but it was more apparent this time. I asked Father Schall how long he has been dealing with the difficulty of drinking. He told me that the doctor diagnosed him with jaw cancer in Spring 2010, and the cancer was operated on in June of 2010. Then it took six months for the whole jaw replacement, new dentures, and healing of the bone graft. He was not able to take liquid into his mouth any longer after the surgery.

Our food arrived, and we started our lunch and slowly switched the topic of conversation. "So, you will have a long trip this December?" asked Father Schall.

"Yes, I am going to Sydney for a workshop on the first ten years of the Indonesian Constitutional Court. The workshop is a combined event between the University of New South Wales and the University of Sydney. I am one of the invited speakers. Do you have anybody in mind that you think I should see in Sydney?"

"One of the sharpest minds in the Australian Catholic Church is no other than the current Archbishop of Sydney, Anthony Fisher. You should see him."

I immediately clarified that I'd meant to ask if Father Schall had any friends in Sydney he recommended I visit. I had no idea that he would recommend me to see Archbishop Fisher; plus who am I to see the Archbishop! Father Schall then promised to send me a few names of whom I could contact.

Father Schall continued, "You are planning to go back home after Australia?"

"Yes, I am planning to go back to Indonesia after the workshop. This trip will be my first visit to Indonesia in five years since I entered the Novitiate."

I then explained to Father Schall that I hadn't been home in the last five years because my parents told me not to come back because it shamed them that their son chose to become a priest. I did not want to fight with them, so I decided not to go home. But recently, my mother became very ill and was hospitalized for heart failure and lung infection. My dad suddenly sent a message via my sister. He asked me to come home and visit my mom, implying that I was an unfilial son for not being home. It seemed strange to me because first they asked me not to come home, but then, blamed me for not being present during my mother's illness. Indeed, guilt was the only emotion that my parents usually imposed upon me. Since I was going to Australia, which was close to Indonesia, I thought perhaps it was time for me to go home to visit my sick mom. I feared that a conflict might escalate during my visit, but I decided to go back anyway.

"I hope that your home visit will be smooth. I am sure that your parents will be proud of you, especially when you will have presented a paper at a conference in Australia. Not many Jesuit Scholastics are invited to give a talk as you have been," said Father Schall.

"Well, that's precisely the problem; they are never proud of me despite all of my achievements."

"It's sad to hear about it, but I will pray for your reconciliation with your parents," said Father Schall.

We finished our lunch, and Father Schall said that he would pay for our meal. He took some cash from his pocket and paid for lunch. He then put all his money in a metal money clip and shared a story:

"When I left Georgetown, the Jesuit community gave me three hundred dollars cash with this clip as my farewell gift. Then I moved to Los Gatos; a few months later, I found that the money is gone, but the clip was still there. I am afraid that someone stole my money, but I did not want to report it to the Superior because I might have forgotten that I already spent the money. I didn't want to falsely accuse the staff in Los Gatos of stealing money if it turned out that I was the one who spent it."

I didn't know what to say to this story, which showed Father Schall's kindness in that he preferred to lose a gift rather than falsely accuse the staff. The story was also humbling because it showed how Father Schall gracefully accepted the possible mental diminishment of ageing. We left the restaurant and I drove Father Schall back to Los Gatos. I said goodbye to him, expressing my wish to see him after my return from Australia and Indonesia. He wished me a good trip and promised to pray for me. I said Happy early Thanksgiving and took off in the van back to Santa Clara.

Christmas in Indonesia

Fatherhood as the Core of the Universe

I left for Sydney via Los Angeles in early December. The workshop in Sydney went well. I was grateful to my friend Rosalind Dixon from the University of New South Wales, who invited me to the workshop and to present my paper. There were several highlights of my visit to Australia. First, I was inspired by ideas from the conference on the idea of the Heroic Court, which later became the topic of my first book. Second, I stayed with the Australian Jesuits in a community that attached to St. Aloysius College in Milson Point. The House is situated in the shadow of the Sydney Harbor Bridge, with a view of the famous Opera House from one of the balconies. On my last day in Sydney, I spent all my money on a ticket to see a show at the Sydney Opera House. I never tried to make an appointment to see Archbishop Anthony Fisher, as Father Schall had suggested. Nevertheless, I visited St. Mary's Cathedral; I attended a daily Mass and prayed there.

After Sydney, I left for Jakarta and stayed in a Jesuit community in the Northern Jakarta region. My mom had been discharged from the hospital for several weeks, but she had to come back to Jakarta for medical checkups. My parents lived on an island, which was located about 45 minutes by plane from the capital city, Jakarta. But as they were still ashamed of my decision to be a priest, they did not want me to come back home. So they decided to fly to Jakarta to see me.

The meeting with my parents was much better than I expected. I was expecting there would be fights or conflict during my visit, but while there was still some tension, at least we could communicate, and they were willing to see me. I believe in the power of hope and prayer; I am not giving up hope and continue to pray that someday my parents can really understand and support my decision to be a priest.

I only stayed for a few weeks in Indonesia as I had to fly back to the U.S. before the Winter quarter began. Nevertheless, there were a few highlights from my short trips. First, I was accompanying my mom on her visits to her doctor. In the hospital waiting room, I used my time to read a book, Alice von Hildebrand's *Memoirs of a Happy Failure.* In this book, Lady Alice shared a story of how she had to face many "sacred frustrations" along the way since her youth. She survived the terror of World War II and ventured to America. After completing her Ph.D. in philosophy at Fordham University, she was repeatedly turned down by Catholic colleges that did not accept women as philosophy teachers. She ended up in an unexpected place, Hunter College. Then she went into detail about her 37 years of teaching at the secular Hunter College, and the trouble she experienced in its anti-Christian environment. She became an adjunct, but after many years of teaching, she received no promotion and no medical coverage. After 11 years, she became an instructor, but at the lowest possible salary on the scale. Miraculously, she was given tenure. Then she became a successful and popular teacher because she was the only person in the philosophy department and perhaps the whole college who stood for the objectivity of truth. Through her teaching, she was able to awaken many students who were longing for truth. Despite having a difficult life, Lady Alice said God supported her through every challenge.

Having read the book, Lady Alice's experience resonated with me. My life had not been an easy life either, as I had to face many challenges along the way. My regency assignment at Santa Clara University had not been easy either. I didn't know how the Province would evaluate me; they might see me as a failed regent. The terrible teaching evaluation might haunt me for the rest of my life. But amid the frustrations and uncertainty, I know that God supported me along the way. I hoped that someday I could look back to my experience at Santa Clara and consider it as part of the memoir of my happy failures.

I brought many books with me to read because I had a long flight to Sydney, Jakarta, and then back to California. One of the books that I brought with me was by C.S Lewis, *George MacDonald: An Anthology*. I picked the book based on the recommendation of Father Schall. Interestingly, in his preface, Lewis wrote that an almost perfect relationship with his father was the earthly root of all of McDonald's wisdom. Lewis wrote further that McDonald learned from his father that "Fatherhood must be at the core of the universe." McDonald saw that religion was basically about the relation of Father and Son as the most central relationship. Here, McDonald did not only talk about the specific relationship between Jesus and His Father but also the Father-Son relationship in general. Our relationship with our father will, in some way, influence our relationship with God. Lewis believed that McDonald learned this wisdom from his father, who was a remarkable man – a man hard and tender, and humorous all at once, in the old fashion of Scotch Christianity.

Lewis's words about MacDonald made me reflect on the relationship with my dad. The rocky relationship with my dad had indeed created a long-lasting impact on my relationship with God. It was hard for me to have a close relationship with God the Father because I never had a real father figure. My dad was mostly absent from parenting, and he let my mom control everything in the house. He only cared about his farm and wanted me to help him on the farm all the time. Therefore, in my relationship with God, I could relate better to Jesus as a friend than to God as a father.

But in retrospect, I could understand my father and should not blame him entirely. My dad grew up in a large family with his twelve siblings. As a middle child, my dad was an abandoned child. My grandfather was away all the time for work as he had to feed his 13 children while my grandmother was busy caring for the younger children. Under these circumstances, my dad did not have any point of reference for fatherhood. Consequently, he did not know his role as a father.

Nevertheless, I also understood that my father was the person who helped form who I am today. When I was young, I did not find something that I was seeking from my father, and so I searched for meaning somewhere else. I found the student movement as a place where I can find meaning, and so my activism was also rebellion against my father. Similarly, my intellectual pursuit came partly from my search for an identity that was different from my father. I did not want to be like my dad, who only had a fifth-grade education. So, I tried to chase my academic dreams and ambitions.

But the next question was whether I could be a good priest and father figure for many since I did not have a good relationship with my dad. While in Indonesia, I went to see a movie with some Indonesian Jesuit Scholastics, *Exodus: Gods and Kings*, with Christian Bale starring as Moses. The movie is spiritually flat, especially in its portrayal of an annoyed little boy as God on Mount Sinai. Nevertheless, the figure of Moses gave me hope about my future role as a spiritual father. Moses had no father figure either; he never knew his biological father. Perhaps the closest father figure for him was his father-in-law, Reuel (Jethro). But Moses served as a father figure to the entire Hebrew people after they escaped from Egypt. He loved them and helped to discipline them, and at the same time, provided for them. I don't want to compare myself to a larger-than-life character like Moses, and I don't think that I will be like Moses. But at least he shows modern day fathers and me that the overwhelming tasks of fatherhood (biological or spiritual) can be achieved when we stay close to God.

There were two moments of interaction with my dad during my short trip that made me reflect more about our relationship. One evening, my dad, my mom, my sister, and I went to the birthday dinner of my uncle who turned 80 years old. There was a massive traffic jam because of heavy rainfall in Jakarta. Jakarta traffic, in general, is already chaotic because the sheer number of vehicles is too great, and the available roads can't provide enough space for all of them. When a heavy rainfall comes, the traffic gets worse because the visibility is bad and vehicles tend to move slower. Slower cars overcrowd intersections and often bring traffic to a halt.

After the party, I was trying to find a taxi for us to get home, but most of the taxi drivers refused to take us because of our destination. In most prominent cities in the United States, cabbies aren't allowed to turn away passengers because of their destination, but there is no such rule in Indonesia. The longer route that the taxi driver must go, the longer they would be stuck in traffic, so they declined to take us after I gave them the destination. Having witnessing several taxis turned me down, my dad jumped in and said, "What's wrong with you that you can get even one taxi for us!" Ronald Richardson, with his family system theory, explains that there are several types of emotional reactions that arise out of unresolved emotional attachment, such as rebelliousness and power struggles.[21] These kinds of emotional reactions are a psychological defense mechanism. As part of my defense mechanism, I immediately reacted to my dad's statement. I felt that my dad was just repeating his statement to me when I was young that I was just a "useless boy." So we had a little fight that night; basically, I defended myself and stated that my dad should not blame me for failing to get a taxi.

A few days after the eventful evening, my parents were preparing for their trip back to their home. On their last day in Jakarta, I was planning to visit them and stay overnight at my sister's apartment where they were staying. I was spending the afternoon with my cousin. I told my parents that I would come to my sister's residence before dinner. My sister was staying at home because she was not feeling well. I arrived before dinner as I promised, then we had a simple dinner; the evening went by without any drama whatsoever. On the following morning, I dropped my parents off at the airport

---

[21] Ronald Richardson, *Becoming a Healthier Pastor: Family Systems Theory and the Pastor's Own Family.* (Minneapolis: Fortress Press, 2005), 15.

by taxi. Surprisingly, my sister told me afterward that my dad wanted to do a little shopping on the day before. But my sister could not accompany her because she was not feeling well. My sister suggested my dad to ask me to accompany him, but he never asked for my help. My dad said that I was too busy with my cousin. I was puzzled by what I heard from sister; if my dad asked me directly, of course, I would have been happy to accompany him. But how could I know he needed help when he never asked me? I did spend time with my cousin in the afternoon, but I could have shortened my visit if I knew that my dad needed a little help. I didn't understand why my dad never asked me to help him; maybe he was too prideful or too reluctant to ask for help from his son.

Christmas day came a few days later; I went to Mass at a local church with my sister. The priest was preaching about Pope Francis' Christmas address to the Roman Curia, the so-called "curial diseases." He focused on the disease of hoarding and tied the issue with the life of the parishioners. I was not interested in hearing a message about hoarding. Instead, my mind was wandering to the passage from the Prologue of John's Gospel, which was the Gospel reading for the Christmas morning mass.

The idea of Incarnation in the prologue of John Gospel is about God's love for humanity. In the world where there is evil, wickedness, and selfishness, God could have come to destroy evil and punish those who work in darkness. But God chose to show His love for us by sending his Only Begotten Son, Jesus. Jesus, as the Son of God, came to the world precisely because He wants to show God's love directly to us. How consoling it is to have a father who loves us and who understands us! My dad might say that he loved me, but he didn't know to express his love, and he didn't have a point of reference for fatherly love. But I had to admit that I have difficulties in understanding or in experiencing my dad's love for me. Maybe this is a kind disease for many modern men who have problems with understanding or experiencing God's love in their lives. On that Christmas day, I just prayed that hopefully, many young men would realize the importance of fatherhood. That they would become good fathers, who could show their love for their children so that their children could also experience and understand God's love for them.

I left Jakarta a few days after Christmas; it was the Feast of Holy Family. On that morning, I prayed over the first reading of the day, from the book of Sirach:

> God sets a father in honor over his children;
> a mother's authority he confirms over her sons.
> Whoever honors his father atones for sins,
> and preserves himself from them.
> When he prays, he is heard;
> he stores up riches who reveres his mother.
> Whoever honors his father is gladdened by children,
> and, when he prays, is heard.
> Whoever reveres his father will live a long life;
> he who obeys his father brings comfort to his mother.

In my prayer, I just asked forgiveness from God for failing to honor my father. I hoped that God would still listen to my prayers and give me a long life, despite the fact that I rarely gave deep respect to my father.

The Thirteenth Saturday

On the Fatherhood of God

Considering the time difference between Indonesia and the United States, I arrived safely in the US on the same day as when I left Jakarta. After resting for a few days, I went to see Father Schall in Los Gatos on the second Saturday of 2015. After checking into the nurse station, I went directly to Father Schall's room and knocked on his door. "Come in," he said. After letting me sit on the chair, Father Schall immediately asked me, "How was your visit to your parents?" I told Father Schall that the visit was much better than I expected despite the lingering tension between us. Then he asked, "How is your mom's health?" I told him that she had recovered and seemed on the right track to full recovery. I thought that she would be fine and so I decided not to stay too long there. "Well, you have your own life here," said Father Schall.

Father Schall's statement made me pause for a second and reflect on my relationship with my parents. I must humbly acknowledge that there was a tendency for me to stay far away from my family because of the rocky relationship between my parents and me. Also, I moved to the United States partly because I wanted to get away from all the family drama. Nevertheless, there was also a guilty feeling in my heart for being a thousand miles away from Indonesia. My extended family and people in my village blamed me for being a unfilial son. Of course, my mom also played on this guilty feeling that being the eldest son, I had the responsibility of taking care of the family. My family is traditionally Confucian, so filial piety is vital. Being a filial son meant complete obedience to one's parents during their lifetime, and as they grew old, I must take the best possible care of them to make sure they were comfortable in every aspect of life, including food, accommodation, and clothing. After the parents' death, the eldest son was required to perform ritual sacrifices at their gravesite, and this was considered to be the most important expression and exercise of filial piety. Therefore, dying without the presence of your son was one of the worst offenses against the concept of filial piety. My parents converted to Catholicism in their 50s, but they were Confucian most of their adult life. In many ways, Confucius's DNA was still in their blood. So, in some way or another, they considered me as an unfilial son.

Father Schall's statement gave me some assurance that it should be ok for me to be a thousand miles away from my parents. In other words, I should not succumb to a guilty feeling for not being close to my parents. But after listening to my reflection, Father Schall made another statement quite surprising to me, given that filial piety has more or less been taken for granted by many people these days. He pointed out if we tell a young man or young woman in the 21st century that God is the Father, they might have difficulty loving God as their Father.

Well, that was precisely the issue that I had been struggling with my whole adult life. I could have a warm and close relationship with Jesus as my friend, but my relationship with God the Father seemed a bit remote. I used to have difficulties relating to God the Father, but after my conversion and my entrance to the religious life, I began to have a relationship with the Father. One of the reasons is that St.

Ignatius of Loyola in his Spiritual Exercises asks us to make colloquy with God the Father. But still, in my default, I tend to go to Jesus in my private or daily prayers.

Father Schall, however, reminded me that we should not necessarily learn about God by analogy from earthly fatherhood. But instead, the opposite, that by learning to know God the Father, we will understand our fathers. While the filial piety is important to help someone to appreciate the love of God the Father, one must not wait till they understand their earthly father before learning about God the Father.

"Have you ever read John Paul II's Catechesis on God the Father?" asked Father Schall.

"Honestly, I never heard about it."

"The Pope gave a series of talks at the General Audiences when he asked us to devote the final year of the 20th century to God the Father."

"I had no idea that 1999 was the year of God the Father."

"Were you living on earth or another planet so that you never heard about it?"

"1999 was the heyday of my political activism and I was still in the wilderness of faith, and so I never heard of it."

Father Schall smiled and continued, "Read about it, and you will learn more about God the Father."

Father Schall explained further that God gradually revealed His Fatherhood to us, culminating with Jesus. We can learn about God the Father through Jesus because, from our understanding of Trinity, Jesus was begotten of the Father. So knowing Jesus means knowing the Father.

"You already have a good relationship with Jesus, so you will certainly have a good relationship with the Father, although you may not realize it," said Father Schall.

"I hope so. But I am still thinking about filial piety. The Fourth Commandment says that we must honor our Father and Mother. And this Commandment is given by God. Being far away from my parents and not being able to take care of them seems to mean that I am breaking God's commandment."

Father Schall answered my question by pointing out that by believing in Jesus as the Son, God the Father assured us about His care for us and communicated His life to us by making us His children through His Son. So, through Jesus, we become the adopted children of God.

"What you are doing now is following His Son in the least Society. So don't feel bad that you cannot take care of your parents as they would like you to. One thing you can do is to ask God to take care of your parents." Father Schall stopped for a moment and asked, "What time is it now?"

It was already lunchtime, so we ended the conversation and moved to the dining room. We sat at a big table with some other Jesuits, so we did not have any further private conversation during lunch.

After lunch, I said goodbye to Father Schall. As usual, he walked with me to my car. I was hoping to visit him soon, and he assured me that he did not have any travel plans so I could visit him any given Saturday.

The Fourteenth Saturday

On Edith Stein and a Retired Philosopher

With the new quarter and a new obligation at the Drahman Advising Center, I did not have a chance to visit Father Schall immediately. It was already the first Saturday of February when I finally went back to Los Gatos. Since I had not had a chance to talk with Father Schall for a couple of weeks, I decided to come earlier to have more time to chat with him. Initially, Father Schall asked me to walk outside to enjoy the sunny winter of California. But while we were coming down to the first floor of the infirmary, Father Schall changed his mind and said, "There is someone that I want you to meet." We went inside the infirmary and visited a Jesuit from the Oregon Province who just moved there, Father James Reichmann. At that time, the California and Oregon Provinces were still two separate entities. Although I was doing my regency assignment in the California Province, I was technically still a member of the Oregon Province. The California and Oregon Provinces later became the new province of Jesuits West in July 2017. Presumably, knowing that I was a member of the Oregon Province, Father Schall wanted to introduce me to Father Reichmann.

Father Reichman was a longtime philosophy professor at Seattle University. He served as a professor of philosophy, department chair, and, finally, emeritus for 43 years. He retired in 2013 and subsequently moved to Los Gatos in 2015. I had known Father Reich-

man a little bit, especially during my early days in the Society of Jesus. Father Reichman welcomed us to his room, which was quite big.
He was sitting on his lazy chair. I sat on the other chair in his room
and Father Schall sat on the bed. Father Schall then introduced me
to Father Reichman as a Jesuit regent from the Oregon Province
who was currently doing a regency at Santa Clara.

I told Father Reichmann that we met several times in the past,
particularly when I was a Jesuit novice. Our first meeting was at the
Jesuit summer villa in Hayden Lake, Idaho. Every summer, the Jesuits of Oregon Province usually have their r&r at the villa. So, from
the baby Jesuits to the elderly, Jesuits got together at around the
same time. When I met Father Reichmann for the first time, there
two things that I remembered. First, he brought a suitcase of full
books with him. Second, he was a type of traditional Jesuit. One afternoon, I happened to sit on the same table with him, and we ended
up discussing liturgy. I remembered Father Reichmann saying that
he did not like the *Novus Ordo* because it focused too much on the
priest, while in the Tridentine Mass, everybody was actively worshipping God.

On that summer, Father Reichmann fell on the dock near the
lake and broke his glasses and had to leave the villa early. I mentioned the incident, but Father Reichmann had no recollection of
the event that summer. When I met him in Los Gatos, Father Reichman was already 92 years old, and I did not expect him to remember
a small incident that summer. But considering he was a philosopher,
perhaps I could revive his memory about our philosophical discussion. I tried to recall our encounter in Summer of 2012 when I just
finished my first year of philosophy studies at Loyola University of

Chicago. That summer, I visited Seattle U and stayed for a couple of days. On one morning, while eating breakfast, I shared with the then Rector of the Jesuit community of Seattle U, Father Pat Howell, that philosophy was a boring subject and I did not see any value in learning philosophy. Father Howell then said to Father Reichman, who sat across the table, "Hi Jim, this young man said that philosophy is boring, and there is no value of studying philosophy." Father Reichmann immediately stopped his breakfast, said, "You cannot be a competent theologian without philosophy."

"I don't have any aspiration to be a theologian, I just want to be a priest," I replied.

"You can be an Imam or Rabbi without philosophy but not a priest without philosophy."

"How about the Israelites in the Old Testament? They were God's chosen people, but they never learned philosophy."

"Oh, they knew philosophy because they made a statement of truth about Yahweh," said Father Reichman with full confidence.

Of course, Father Reichman had no recollection at all about our encounter that summer. Then, I made my last attempt to refresh his memory. "Father Reichman, did you remember that summer you were working on the article about Edith Stein?" After our encounter that morning, Father Reichman told me he was writing about Edith Stein, a German Jewish philosopher who converted to Catholicism and became a Discalced Carmelite nun. Father Reichman enthusiastically shared with me about his work on Edith Stein, like a man finding a treasure. First, there are not many people who were studying Edith Stein yet. Second, Edith Stein herself was a great philosopher who could combine phenomenology and Thomistic philosophy. Edith Stein was a protégé of Edmund Husserl, the Father of Phenomenology. But after her conversion to Catholicism, she began to move into the phase of scholastic philosophy. In 1925, Edith Sein translated Aquinas' *Disputed Questions about Truth*, and then she began to write two treaties on Aquinas: *Potency and Act*, a study of the central concepts developed by Thomas Aquinas, and *Finite and Eternal Being*, which discusses Aquinas from a phenomenological point of view.

The summer we met in Seattle U, Father Reichman was finishing his article, which turned out to be his last article, on *Edith Stein, Thomas Aquinas, and the Principle of Individuation*.[22] Sadly, Father Reichman did not remember his last article on Edith Stein, let alone our encounter. I was still curious why he failed to recall his last article, but assumed that his memory was failing, despite his ability to communicate well. I had hoped we could further discuss Edith Stein, but Father Reichman was interested in another topic.

"Did you study at Seattle U? I just received news that Seattle U received 12 million dollars in donations. A longtime friend of Seattle U donated the money to support the Jesuit Catholic character of SU's education."

Father Schall interjected and said, "No, he went to graduate school at the University of Washington and earned his Ph.D. there. Do you know how the Seattle U is going to use the money?"

---

[22] James B. Reichmann, S.J., "Edith Stein, Thomas Aquinas, and the Principle of Individuation," *American Catholic Philosophical Quarterly*, Volume 87, Issue 1, Winter 2013.

"I heard that some of it would go to the Institute for Catholic Thought and Culture, and the bigger chunk of the gift will provide scholarships for students."

Father Schall did not seem interested in pursuing a further conversation about Seattle U, and neither did I. He switched the topic by asking Father Reichman, "Did you bring many of your philosophy books here?" As far as I could see, he had not brought many books with him. The bookshelf was pretty much empty, with only a few books.

Father Reichman replied, "I just brought a few books that I wrote." He stood up and picked up two books from the bookshelf. The first book was *Philosophy of the Human Person*[23] and the second book was *Evolution, Animal Rights, and the Environment.* [24] Father Schall was more interested in the second book. I was also curious about the second book because I wondered what a philosopher like Father Reichman had to say about animal rights and the environment. The cover of the book was also interesting because it had a big picture of a chimpanzee on it.

"Tell us more about this book, Jim?" asked Father Schall.

Father Reichmann explained that in the book, he argued against the effort to build a case for animal and environmental rights. The point of departure of the book was that before assigning rights to animals and the environment, we must be very clear about *"what is"*

---

[23] James B. Reichmann, *Philosophy of the Human Person.* (Chicago: Loyola University Press, 1985).

[24] James Reichmann, *Evolution, Animal Rights, and the Environment.* (Washington DC: Catholic University of America Press, 2000).

it we are mapping and *to whom* and *why*. Father Reichman then investigated the difference between human and nonhuman animals in terms of knowing, communicating, and doing. The bottom line is that he argued any effort to build a case for animal and environmental rights resting on a Darwinian evolutionary theory would likely fail.

"This book is interesting! I want to read it. May I borrow it?" asked Father Schall.

Father Reichman did not mind letting Father Schall borrow his book. Again, I was amazed that an elderly priest like Father Schall was still interested in more in-depth study.

Father Reichman suddenly said, "I received the news this morning that a long-term benefactor donated 12 million donations to Seattle U. This donation will strengthen the Catholic character of the University."

"You already told us about the news, Jim," said Father Schall.

When I heard that Father Reichmann repeated his statement, I knew that he struggled with memory loss. He told us the news a few minutes ago, but he could not remember what he said.

"Have I told you about the news in the *San Francisco Chronicle* this morning?" asked Father Reichmann.

"No, what's the story?"

"The *Chronicle* criticizes the Archbishop for issuing guidance for Catholic school teachers' moral behavior. I could not believe that they criticized the Archbishop for asking its teachers to honor church teachings."

In early February 2015, the Archbishop of San Francisco, Salvatore Cordileone, released the Archdiocese's new high school teachers' handbook, in which he calls staff members — in their professional and private lives — to honor church teachings. He specifically cited opposition to abortion, contraception, homosexuality, artificial insemination, cloning, and same-sex marriage, not to mention masturbation, fornication, and pornography.

"You better believe it! This is the world we live in now," said Father Schall.

"Don't they know in Catholic schools, students should be educated in the Catholic faith?"

"What they think of first is 'tolerance,' not the truth. If you disagree with their world view, you will be accused of bigotry and intolerance."

Father Schall paused for a moment and continued, "Have you ever heard the story of a florist in Seattle who refused to provide flowers for a same-sex wedding? The state not only went after her business but also sued her personally and threatened to bankrupt her. So, you'd better believe the story in the *Chronicle*."

We finished our conversation on that note; we said goodbye to Father Reichmann and walked to the dining room for lunch. We joined some other Jesuits for lunch, so I did not have a chance to talk privately with Father Schall. We finished our lunch; as usual, Father Schall walked with me to my car. While we were walking, Father Schall asked me a question, "From your conversation with Jim, you seem interested in Edith Stein." I replied, "I credited her as a person who helped me with my philosophy studies." When Father Reichmann shared with me about his writing project on Edith Stein in

2012, I was still struggling with philosophy studies. At the end of the summer, I made my 8-day silent retreat at Gonzaga Jesuit community in Spokane, Washington. The sixth day of my retreat was the feast of St. Edith Stein. During the daily mass at the community chapel, Fr. Brad Reynolds, a Jesuit who was celebrating the Mass, compared the life of Edith Stein with her cohort, Martin Heidegger. Both were disciples of Edmund Husserl. Heidegger was quite successful in his academic life and later was appointed to the rector position at the University of Freiburg. Heidegger grew up as a Catholic but distanced himself from the Catholic faith in his late twenties, and later he built some collaboration with Nazis. In contrast, Husserl did not support Edith Stein's appointment to the University of Freiburg because she was a woman. After her endeavors for securing a professorship were in vain, Edith Stein joined the Carmelite Convent.

My discussion with Father Reichmann and Father Reynolds' homily opened my eyes to realize that I had a good friend, St. Edith Stein, who had been praying for me throughout my philosophy studies. After my 8-day retreat, I went back to Chicago and resumed my philosophy studies. Back in school, I began to read many philosophical writings of St. Edith Stein and indeed, she helped to kindle my interest in studying philosophy. By the end of my philosophy study, thanks to St. Edith Stein, I developed a great interest in studying philosophy. Edith Stein extended her support and prayers during my studies, and I hope that she will continue to pray for me in my journey as a Jesuit. I knew that Edith Stein was an excellent teacher when she held an adjunct position, teaching German and history at the Dominican Sisters' school and teacher training college of St. Magdalen's Convent in Speyer. She was well beloved by her students. I hoped that she could also pray for me to become a good teacher. Perhaps my predicament at Santa Clara was because I had forgotten to ask her intercession.

"Keep praying and asking her intercession, she will help you, and don't forget to ask the intercession of Saint Claire," said Father Schall.

We finished our conversation and I said goodbye to Father Schall, promising that I would come to visit him soon. Then I drove back to Santa Clara.

The Fifteenth Saturday

On the Joys and Hopes at Our Lady's University

I wish that I could have visited Father Schall every Saturday, but I was still struggling to manage my work and schedule, and so often I had to work on Saturday. It was already the first Saturday of March when I finally came back to Los Gatos. There was also a sad feeling within me because I knew that I didn't have much time left. My regency assignment would over in the summer, and I was waiting for the next assignment. I felt I should try to maximize my time with Father Schall.

As usual, I checked in at the Nursing Station and then went to the second floor. I knocked at Father Schall's room, and he let me in. After I sat down, he asked me if anything exciting was happening in my life.

"I am going to the University of Notre Dame in a few weeks to present my paper at the 50th Anniversary of *Gaudium Et Spes*."

"Good to hear that you have an opportunity to present your paper at Notre Dame."

Father Schall stopped for a few seconds and continued, "What's your paper about?"

"My paper is about the Catholic Vision of Work, Pregnancy, and Equality."

Father Schall did not seem interested to hear about my paper; he just replied, "I hope that you will have a good experience at Notre Dame. It's a good place to visit."

"So, Father Schall," I asked, "what do you think about *Gaudium et Spes*?"

"What time is it now? Why don't we have lunch and discuss *Gaudium et Spes*?"

It was quite close to lunchtime, so we moved to the dining room and sat privately to resume our conversation. I continued the conversation by asking, "Father Schall, what do you think about Jacques Maritain influence on *Gaudium et Spes*?"

From my research, I knew that Maritain was one of the most influential thinkers behind Vatican Council II. In 1936, Maritain published his seminal book, *Integral Humanism*, which provided a philosophical framework for the project of synthesizing the Liberal and Thomist traditions. *Integral Humanism* later profoundly influenced the formulation of *Gaudium et Spes*.[25] The influence of Maritain's *Integral Humanism* on *Gaudium et Spes* can be traced back to the friendship between Maritain and Monsignor Giovanni Battista Montini, who later became Pope Paul VI. It was not clear when they both met for the first time, but Montini had a long standing interest in Maritain's work.[26] Peter Hebblethwaite, the biographer of Pope Paul VI, said, "Maritain provided Montini and his friends with a vision of a 'Christian civilization,' a 'new Christendom'.... What was 'new' about Maritain's Christendom was that it was lay rather than

---

[25] Jacques Maritain. *Integral Humanism: Temporal and Spiritual Problems of a New Christendom* (New York: Scribner, 1968)

[26] Peter Hebblethwaite. *Paul VI: The First Modern Pope.* (New York: Paulist Press, 1993), 121

clerical democratic, rather than authoritarian." [27] In 1960, Archbishop Montini used Maritain's arguments in *Integral Humanism* in his presentation to the Commission preparing for Vatican Council II.[28] After the death of Pope John XIII, Cardinal Montini, now Pope Paul VI, presided over the Council and invoked Maritain's work.

"The problem with Maritain is that he was too optimistic about his project," said Father Schall.

Father Schall then explained that Maritain understood that there are two kinds of Humanism. The first theory of Humanism comes from classical and revelational tradition, which recognizes God as the center of man. It is based on natural law and natural rights, inspired by Gospel teaching about love for neighbor and human dignity. The second theory understands human beings as "self-sufficient" creatures, centered on themselves and not bound by anything but their own wills. Maritain had hoped that the former view would come to prevail after the world saw the brutality of World War II and the rise of the totalitarian Marxist regime. Maritain did not think that the latter view, which originated in Hobbes, Rousseau, and Nietzsche, would come to dominate the classical understanding, but he was wrong in his assessment.

Father Schall explained further that although Maritain did not fully embrace the man-centered world view, he wanted to establish a project that recognizes that there is a human purpose in the world, and it can be achieved by human action. He proposed a new way to relate to the temporal and the eternal. But essentially, it is a temporal

---

[27] Ibid. p. 122.
[28] Ibid. p. 605.

project, subject to change by some political and cultural configurations that adhere to some higher principle. But Maritain overestimated of the possibilities of the temporal project overpowering the eternal project, with people only looking to their own will as its end.

Father Schall moved on to point out that in *Gaudium Et Spes*, we will find a discussion of the modern world and modern man. The document discusses various ways modern men tried to combine different philosophies to avoid confronting the human condition, including suffering and death. Some want to find the solutions in man's own efforts, and some just despair in finding answers. Basically, everyone lives in their self-made world. Like Maritain, *Gaudium et Spes* is too optimistic in dealing with the modern world. The document calls the Church to be more adaptive to the modern world, not merely making use of modern technology but also appropriating certain social, political, cultural, and values of the modern age. But it overestimates the forces of modernity, with its self-made man worldview, and how this can easily overshadow the God-made world view that is based on the classical and biblical tradition.

Father Schall switched the topic of conversation by asking, "Are you planning to do anything else while in Notre Dame?"

"I don't have any plans other than attending the conference; it will be my first visit to Notre Dame and I don't know anybody there. But I am planning to fly to DC after I visit Notre Dame. The Provincial asked me to explore the CPE (Clinical Pastoral Education) program at Georgetown Hospital for my third year of regency."

"Why is he asking you to do that?"

I then explained that there are at least two reasons. First, the Society of Jesus had moved to adapt the 2+1 formula for regency, in which a regent will do two years of traditional regency like teaching high school or college, and for the third year, he must undergo the so-called poverty apostolate, to work closely with the poor and marginalized. Second, the Provincial thought that I needed to grow in my pastoral ministry, and so he wanted me to explore the CPE program. The Provincial told me, "I want you to have a good bedside manner as a priest."

Father Schall responded, "What's the point of having a good bedside manner, but little medical knowledge? It's fraud. As a priest, you can be very pastoral if you know what you teach. Right now, what you need is to have a solid foundation in the Church's teaching."

"Well, I wish you were my Provincial or my formation director."

"What do you want to do if they gave you a choice?"

"If they give me a choice, I would spend more time writing and researching. I want to turn my dissertation into a book."

"Why don't you ask to do that for your third year of regency?"

"I don't think that they will give me the opportunity."

"How old are you now?"

"I will turn 41 next month."

"You should not waste your time; it will be better for you to study more and prepare yourselves for your work at the University."

"I think that the decision is final that I have to undergo CPE next year."

"Maybe you should check if Notre Dame has an opportunity for you to be a visiting scholar or something. It will be good if you can spend one year there."

"I can try, but again, I don't think the Provincial will approve it."

We finished our serious conversation on that note and then just chatted for the remainder of lunch. After we finished our lunch, as usual, Father Schall walked with me toward my car. While we were walking, I asked Father Schall, "do you have any thoughts about the poverty apostolate for the third year of regency?"

"Give me a break!" he exclaimed. "The issue is not whether the poor ought to be helped or accompanied either by a priest or community organizer. But the question is how does one bring the poor to a situation where they can help themselves. We are spending many years of our Jesuit education precisely to learn how to bring the poor to help themselves."

"Yeah, I also I think that it will be better for me to focus on my theological studies at this moment. Plus, I already spent my childhood in poverty; I did not grow up with running water and electricity in my village. So I already have had firsthand experience of poverty."

"You must tell your story to the Provincial."

Father Schall paused for a moment and continued, "Right now, I am finishing a book, which argues that the solution to poverty is not about how much we can give to the poor, what they want or need. But it is how we can make it possible for the poor to become more productive. I want to help the poor by thinking of the best way to create a situation where they can help themselves."[29]

"Sounds like an interesting book! I look forward to reading it."

---

[29] The book was later published as *On Christians and Prosperity* (Grand Rapids, Michigan: Acton Institute, 2015).

We finished our conversation on that note; I said goodbye to Father Schall, and I promised to visit him after my trip to Notre Dame. Father Schall wished me a good trip and said, "May you find the joys and the hopes at Notre Dame!" In his old age, he had not lost his sense of humor. The joys and the hopes are indeed the literal meaning of *Gaudium et Spes*; he was playing with the words to tease me.

The Sixteenth Saturday

On Augustine Deformed

The trip to Notre Dame and DC was quite eventful. But I got extremely sick with a cold at the end of the journey. Maybe I caught a bug on the plane or perhaps because of the weather change, as it was snowing in Notre Dame. I had been away from Chicago for almost two years so my body could not bear the brutality of the Midwest winter any longer. After I barely made the trip home, I rested for a few days to recover. Then the Easter came and was followed by a new spring quarter. It was already the second Saturday of April when I had the opportunity to visit Father Schall.

I emailed Father Schall about my plans to visit him, and he replied that he would be there waiting for me. Spring had come, but I did not anticipate that many people would drive to Santa Cruz on a Saturday morning. Usually, it took 20 minutes to drive from Santa Clara to Los Gatos, but that morning, it took me a little more than an hour to get there. I arrived around 10 minutes after midday. After I checked in to the nurses' station, I went to Father Schall's room and knocked, but there was no answer. I guessed that Father Schall might have gone to the dining room for lunch. I went to the dining room and saw Father Schall lining up for lunch. I came to him and apologized for my late arrival. "I thought that you wouldn't show up," he replied.

We found a private table and sat together. Father Schall asked me about my trip. I shared with Father Schall that my paper presentation at Notre Dame went well. The conference itself was well organized, but many dissident theologians attended the conference. Almost of all of them were critical to Pope Emeritus Benedict XVI and condemned him. Some of them were representing Catholic universities, including Jesuit universities. Cardinal Winfried Napier, OFM of Durban, South Africa, was one of the keynote speakers. I spoke briefly with the Cardinal at the conference, and he did not seem happy with the opinion of the dissident theologians.

But I did follow Father Schall's advice in pursuing an opportunity of doing research at Notre Dame. I met with Paolo Carozza, a law professor and the Director of Kellogg Institute for International Studies at Notre Dame. Based on our conversation, Paolo said that there is a possibility for me to come there as a guest scholar in the coming academic year. Also, there was a Catholic hospital about a one-hour drive from South Bend, St. Anthony Hospital, where I could possibly volunteer as part of my apostolic work.[30]

My visit to DC went well; I stayed at the Georgetown Jesuit community and had an interview for an interview program at

---

[30] In 1875, a group of Catholic Sisters from Olpe, Germany, answered a call to bring ministries of health and education to the Midwest United States. The women's religious congregation later became known as the Sisters of St. Francis of Perpetual Adoration, founded St. Anthony Hospital and provided medical services to patients in its longtime location at 301 W. Homer St. In early January of 2019, all the patients there were moved to the Franciscan's new hospital at 3500 Franciscan Way in Michigan City. In 2020, The Franciscan Alliance Board of Directors decided to tear down much of the 400,000 square-foot former hospital.

Georgetown Medstar Hospital. I also made inquiries to Georgetown Law School about the possibility of a visiting position. The CPE program itself was supposed to be part-time, and so I was hoping to do little research and writing on the side.

Father Schall responded to my story, "It's a lot if you want to do both CPE and research."

"I think it's still doable; the CPE will only meet for three and a half days a week, and I can do at least one day for research and writing."

"Trust me. If you want to do research and writing, you must focus your time and energy on your project."

"Yeah, I think that the Notre Dame option is more realistic than the Georgetown one. I can do writing and full-time research, and take a little break 3 -5 hours per week to volunteer at the hospital."

"Talk to the Provincial about it, and hopefully he can understand what is more important to you."

"I will try."

I understood Father Schall to be part of the generation that valued the intellectual apostolate of the Society of Jesus. About a year before, the then-General Superior of the Society of Jesus, Father Adolfo Nicholas, published a letter, *On the Intellectual Apostolate*. Father Nicholas stated that "the long tradition of the involvement of the Society of Jesus in the intellectual apostolate forms part of our religious identity."[31] Father Nicholas issued an invitation to the Society for the intellectual apostolate's renewal, particularly in the field

---

[31] Adolfo Nicholas, *On Jesuits missioned to the intellectual apostolate*, General Curia of the Society of Jesus, May 24, 2014.

of research. Father Schall was quite enthusiastic about reading the letter. In his tribute to the late Jesuit Father John Navone, another one of the intellectual giants of his generation, Father Schall cited Father Nicholas' letter and stated that the intellectual apostolate means "writing, thinking, lecturing, and teaching, something to which John Navone has devoted his life. It is in a way a paradoxical life since so much that is true is rejected as insanity, as Chesterton implied. But this life has its own rewards and pleasures, as I like to put it."[32] Father Schall believed in the intellectual apostolate, and so he tried to encourage me to pursue the intellectual apostolate by proposing to the Provincial that I spend my third year of regency doing research and writing.

Father Schall's statement from our last meeting still intrigued me, that a good doctor with only a good bedside manner is a fraud if he does not have sufficient medical knowledge. So I asked Father Schall to elaborate upon this statement because it could be helpful for me when speaking to my Provincial about my desire to do research and writing for my third year of regency.

As usual, Father Schall responded to my question by referring to something else.

"I am currently reading a book titled *Augustine Deformed*. Have you heard about it?"

"No," I replied.

---

[32] James V. Schall, "On Remembering What We Know: An Illuminating Life." Catholic World Report. May 4, 2014. The initial address was given on April 24th by Father Schall at Gonzaga University (Spokane, WA), at the invitation of the school's Faith and Reason Institute, in honor of Father John Navone, S.J.

"It is a remarkable book, and I highly recommended you read it." Father Schall explained that in one of the chapters of the book, the author, John Rist, invites us to rethink Genesis' account of the Creation and the Fall from Augustine's perspective. Augustine called Adam's condition before the fall as the lesser freedom (*libertas minor*), and the freedom of God and of the saints in heaven as the greater freedom (*libertas maior*). Within the lesser freedom, the unfallen Adam enjoyed some sort of libertarian choice. His lesser freedom entailed that he could not sin, but in exercising his choice, he longed for the autonomous freedom of moral indifference. The unfallen Adam could have chosen the better option of not sinning. But he decided to sin, prompted by the devil, by being disobedient to God.

The drama of unfallen Adam displays a complicated story with the malice of a third party, the devil, who exploits the weakness of Adam's libertarian freedom. The question is, why did God allow Adam to sin? Augustine believed that only God knows why he allowed the possibility of sin. But Augustine thinks that the fall of Adam opens the possibility of a triumphant return of his descendants. The bottom line is that God has established a premise that it is better to bring good from evil than not to allow evil. In other words, God will not allow evil unless He would be able to bring forth good from evil. God then turns the tragedy of the fall into triumph through the Incarnation, in which He saves humanity by sending the Second Person of the Trinity.

Fr. Schall explains further that Rist's invitation to rethink the story of Genesis from Augustinian's perspective reminded him of

Pope Pius XII's 1950 encyclical, *Humani Generis*. "Have you ever read *Humani Generis*?" asked Father Schall.

"Yes, I read it in my Catholic Social Teaching class at Loyola Chicago."

"Well, your formation is not too bad; at least they asked you to read some primary sources."

"I think it depends on the professor; you can get a crappy professor who will assign you crappy stuff, but a professor like Father Bob Araujo assigned us primary resources in our Catholic Social Teaching class."

"Oh, Bob Araujo taught you Catholic Social Teaching? Do you keep in touch with him?"

"Yes, I kept in touch with him after I left Chicago."

"How is he doing? I heard that he is a bad shape because of cancer."

"Yeah, he already stepped down from his Chair as John Courtney Murray professor at Loyola Chicago Law School, and now he is spending his last days at the New England Province Infirmary in Weston, Massachusetts."

"We should keep praying for him." Father Schall paused for a moment and continued, "Do you still remember what *Humani Generis* is about?"

"If I remember correctly, it is about the reasonable character of the Catholic faith. We read it in conjunction with *Fides et Ratio* and *Veritatis Splendor*."

"It's worthwhile to re-read *Humani Generis*. It tells how the Church highly values human reason to demonstrate the foundations of the Catholic faith. But reason can do these jobs safely when it is properly trained by a sound philosophy that has been acknowledged and accepted by the Church in the light of revelation."

Father Schall continued, "*Augustine Deformed* shows us that we must have proper philosophical training to meditate on freedom and evil. So you should remind the Provincial that you will become a more effective priest in evangelization if you have more time to solidify your philosophical knowledge."

"I am not sure I can convince the Provincial that I will be a more effective priest through my philosophy."

"You can point to Cardinal Newman, who showed us our need to be men of mind and intelligence. Newman was amazingly effective in his sermons because he had a solid foundation of philosophy and theology."

"I will try to convince the Provincial about going to Notre Dame for research and writing, but I am pessimistic that he will allow me to do so."

"Even if you fail, you must keep your intellectual interests alive and informed, especially in theology and philosophy."

Father Schall then explained that in his observation, many priests fail to prioritize their intellectual life after ordination. But he believed it was fatal for a priest to underestimate the importance of his intellectual life because a priest must have an intellectual grasp of why Catholicism is true and understand the arguments and practices that deny the foundation of Catholicism.

"Have you ever read St. Augustine's Sermon on Pastors?" asked Father Schall.

"I don't think so."

"You must read it before your ordination."

Father Schall then explained that in that sermon, St. Augustine warned the pastors who failed to strengthen the weak, that is, their flock. The weak need the strength of the strong, but often the pastors are not strong enough because they have failed in their moral and spiritual life. The failure in virtue will eventually lead to the failure of the mind, in which the pastors will experience the intellect's failure. They will turn into wicked and false shepherds who lead their flocks astray instead of preaching the truth.

We finished the conversation on that note as we were finishing our lunch. After lunch, I thanked Father Schall for his wisdom about the necessity of being a learned priest, and he then walked with me to my car. As we walked out the main door of the Sacred Heart Center, Father Schall shared some of his final thoughts:

"I will pray for you that the Provincial can understand the importance of your intellectual work." He paused for a moment and continued, "I think that we (the Jesuits) will be better in our works if we take more time and energy to pursue philosophy and theology seriously and steadily in our lives."

I said goodbye to Father Schall and promised to keep him updated about my conversation with the Provincial. I told him that I had travel plans for another conference in the next few weeks, so I might not be able to see him until early May.

The Seventeenth Saturday

On Solzhenitsyn
& Losing Our Souls at the Best University

Many things had happened since my last visit to Father Schall in April; first, I talked with my formation director and expressed my desire to go to the University of Notre Dame for my third year of regency. Surprisingly, my formation director, Father Sean Michaelson, S.J., said that he would be my advocate, and he was one who talked to the Provincial about my desire. To cut the story short, my Provincial Superior agreed to let me pursue intellectual works at the University of Notre Dame for my third year of regency. After I received the good news, I made new arrangements for my travel plans so that I could visit Notre Dame to solidify my visiting position. I already planned to go to New Haven, Connecticut, for a Freedom of Expression Scholars Conference at Yale Law School. I decided to stop at Notre Dame on my way to New Haven.

I was busy with grading mid-term examinations after the trips to South Bend and New Haven in early May. The undergraduate program at Santa Clara used the quarter system, which ended in June. The students were having their midterms in early May, which enabled me to travel to the conference.

It was already the third Saturday of May when I finally had a chance to visit Father Schall. I emailed Father Schall about my plan to visit, and he replied that he wouldn't be available to meet during lunchtime because his grandniece was planning to take him out to lunch. I then asked him whether there would be a chance to visit at a different time that Saturday. Father Schall said, "Why don't you come for dinner; you don't have dinner anyway at Santa Clara. Dennis and Bill usually come here for dinner, and so you can join them if you like." Indeed, there was no dinner at the Santa Clara University Jesuit community on Saturdays. Father Schall referred to Father Dennis Smolarski, S.J., and Father Bill Rewak, S.J., from Santa Clara Jesuit Community, who usually went to Sacred Heart Center in Los Gatos to have dinner on Saturday evening.

I came earlier on that Saturday to Los Gatos. The Jesuits usually have social time before dinner, so I was hoping to use the social time to chat with Father Schall in case we could not find a private table during dinner. As usual, I checked in to the nursing station and then went to Father Schall's room. I saw that Father Schall was writing something on his computer. Father Schall asked me how I was doing and how was my trip to New Haven.

I told him that I stayed at the Dominican Priory at St. Mary's Church in New Haven. I did not want to spend too much money on a hotel. I reached out to the Dominican Priory and asked if I could stay there during my visit. It was different, staying with the Dominicans, but I was grateful for their generosity.

My visit to Yale Law School itself was not great for different reasons. First, my paper was titled *Hamlet with the Prince: Religious Speech as High-Value Speech in the Culture Wars*. I was scheduled to present a paper on Saturday at 5:15 PM. Interestingly, at 3:30 PM session, Professor Caroline Corbin presented a similar topic to mine, with a paper titled *Speech or Conduct: The Cake Wars*. In some ways, we both were discussing the same issue of some vendors, either bakers, florists, or photographers who declined to serve people who requested service for their same-sex wedding ceremony. My paper was discussing the culture wars and freedom of expression in general, but Professor Corbin specifically discussed cake artists who declined to make a wedding cake for a same-sex couple.

I attended Professor Corbin's session, which was packed and had a lively discussion. But only one participant came to my session and listened to my paper. Perhaps no one knew me. The conference had been in session since 8:30am and my presentation was among the last of the day and everyone was ready to leave. Or perhaps they had had their fill of the topic and discussions of it at Professor Corbin's presentation. Either way, I felt humiliated.

"Don't feel bad about that. You did good research and presented your paper well. At least you can put it on your CV that you presented at Yale Law School. Nobody will ask you how many people listened to your talk," said Father Schall.

But apart from that humiliating experience, I had another depressing experience at Yale Law School. A few years ago, when I was a novice doing my long experiment at the University of San Francisco, I came to know a young lady who was serving on the Jesuit Volunteer Corp in San Francisco. She aspired to go to law school, and I tried to help her by supporting and encouraging her. Over the years, I thought we had become good friends. I got to know her family and she invited me to come to her parents' house for Christmas dinner.

Two years after her service in San Francisco, she was accepted to Yale Law School. When she informed me about her acceptance, she told me, "You should come to visit me at Yale." I replied that as much as I like to visit her, I could not do so easily, because as a Jesuit in training, I needed to ask permission and money from my Superior to travel to visit a friend. But if I had an opportunity to attend a conference or to present a paper, then I had a legitimate reason to visit her. I told her, "Let's have a faith that I will come to visit you at Yale."

We were still in contact after she began her studies at Yale Law School. But after the summer of her first year, she stopped replying to my attempts to stay in touch. I thought she was just busy; I understood that life as a law school student is demanding. When my paper was accepted for the Freedom for Information Scholars Conference, I emailed, texted, and left her a voice message letting her know that I was coming to Yale, and we should plan to get together. I heard nothing from her. I began to wonder why she was ghosting me.

A few days before I left for my trip to New Haven, I called her again and left a message to see if she was interested in getting together. Still, there was no answer. Interestingly, at the conference, during the break between the session, I saw her in the hallway of Sterling Law Building. I greeted her, but she simply replied, "What are you doing here? Are you attending a conference?" I told her I was presenting a paper at the conference, to which she replied, "Ok, please take care of yourself," and walked away.

I was sad to see our friendship end like that. I did not know what I had done wrong and why she treated me like that. Maybe she thought that I had a romantic interest in her. Yet I had acted no differently towards her than I did toward other female friends. I do not know what her main reason for ending our friendship like that.

Overall, my trip to Yale was quite depressing; my paper did not receive a good response, and I lost a friend.

"Reread Aristotle's *Nicomachean Ethics*," said Father Schall in response to my story.

Father Schall reminded me about Aristotle's treatise on friendship in which he explained that we cannot be friends with just anybody. Friendship cannot be coerced because friendship is like love; we can love other persons only if they respond to us. We can possess many good habits and become more loveable to others. Nevertheless, even if we are lovable or good, we should keep in mind that somehow, other people can always refuse to be our friends. As Aristotle said, we can only have a few good friends in this life, perhaps no more than one or two, because we cannot be friends with everybody in any deep sense.

Father Schall further explained that one of the biggest mistakes of modern people is to lower the standard of friendship; we base our relationship with others on the lowest basis, so that everyone could be friends with everyone. But most people remain unknown to each other at the deepest levels.

"Do you think you have a friendship with this young lady in any deep sense?" asked Father Schall.

"Honestly, no. I got to know her maybe only for three months in San Francisco. Then we kept up a correspondence via email, letters, and phone in the past years. She came to visit me in the Novitiate; then I came to visit her family house for Christmas. She came to my first vows ceremony. We met several times over the years when we happened to be in the same city. That's it."

"In that case, she is not a friend in a deep sense. So, no worries about losing her because there was no deep friendship to lose in the first place."

"I understand that, but it's still sad to see the relationship end like that. The irony is that she asked me to visit her at Yale, and then I did visit her, but it was not the kind of reunion that I expected at the best law school in the country."

"Remember that you cannot demand a friendship from her." Father Schall paused for a moment and continued, "Speaking about the best law schools, you should also read more about Solzhenitsyn."

Father Schall picked a book from his desk and showed me a book that he was currently reading, titled *The Other Solzhenitsyn* by Daniel Mahoney. Father Schall asserted that, according to Solzhenitsyn, one could lose his/her soul at the best universities, but it is possible to save one's soul in the worst places on earth, like a concentration camp. Solzhenitsyn reminds us that the time he spent in the gulag was a purifying moment that led him to discover his own soul and a way to God.

"You felt that you were kind of losing your soul at the best law school, but in reality, there are many people losing their souls at institutions like Yale," said Father Schall. He stopped for a moment and continued, "Have you read a lot of Solzhenitsyn?"

"Honestly, no. I read *One Day in the Life of Ivan Denisovich* many years ago. Others than that, I haven't read his works."

"You must certainly read the Gulag Archipelago and his Harvard commencement address."

"Father Schall, what do you think that we can learn from Solzhenitsyn, apart from learning horrifying facts about the Soviet Union.?"

"You wouldn't ask that question if you read a lot of Solzhenitsyn's works."

Father Schall then explained that one of the lessons that we can learn from Solzhenitsyn is intellectual courage. The intellectual courage means that one is willing to speak the unpopular truth. Father Schall pointed out that an intellectual must speak the truth, but the intellectuals often yield to popularity and prestige. In the end, what we have is not intellectual courage, but rather intellectual betrayal.

"If you read his Harvard commencement address, you will understand the virtue of intellectual courage in Solzhenitsyn," said Father Schall.

After pausing for a moment, he continued, "You might prefer to work in a Jesuit university in the future because it is easy for you to live with the Jesuit community. But you must have intellectual courage if you want to work in Jesuit universities these days. Otherwise, you can apply for a job at different Catholic universities like Villanova or Notre Dame. Of course, you still need intellectual courage in those places, but the challenges that you will face are different than in Jesuit universities."

"Oh yes, but Father Schall, I forgot to tell you that the Provincial has approved that I go to Notre Dame next year!"

"This is good news; we must celebrate this evening."

"I still don't know why the Provincial changed his mind, but I am happy that he is letting me pursue intellectual works next year."

"Well, he can still be a reasonable man, so he might see the value of letting you go to Notre Dame to do research and writing. Let us go to dinner now, and celebrate this good news."

We moved to the dining room, which was already crowded with many retired Jesuits who were enjoying their Saturday night meal. We joined a table with some Jesuits who I did not know personally. I visited Los Gatos often in the last year, but I mostly spent my time with Father Schall, and still did not know many of the residents. As usual, Father Schall proudly introduced me to the crowd as a Jesuit regent who was currently teaching at Santa Clara, and next year, going to Notre Dame.

"How did you get to know Jim?" asked one of the retired Jesuits with a Boston accent.

"It's a long story, but to make it short, I had an interest in political philosophy and constitutional politics, so I reached out to Father Schall after he arrived at Los Gatos."

"So, you are also a political science guy?" asked the same priest.

I did not want to complicate the matters, and so I decided neither to deny nor confirm his assumption. I could correct his wrong assumption about me, but it would not be easy to explain my academic background, which did not fit neatly into any academic field.

"He obtained his Ph.D. from the University of Washington," said Father Schall.

The Jesuits with the Bostonian accent continued, "You know that Winston Churchill once said that 'politicians are like diapers. They need to be changed regularly.' So be careful, you guys, with the political scientists!"

"Well, he used those words to describe politicians, which are different from political scientists," Father Schall replied.

"What's the difference? You guys all are the same!"

"Of course, they are different; most of the politicians are not political scientists and vice versa. One of the reasons that the world has many terrible politicians is because they have no clue about political philosophy."

"Well, it does not change the fact that politicians and diapers should be changed often."

"Do you know why they should be changed often?"

"Because they are dirty and disgusting."

"In the ancient world, a member of the royal dynasty inherits the throne either by order of succession or by killing the king. In the modern world, the election is a new way to kill the king. So the new king comes to power by killing the old king in an election."

Our kitchen table conversation seemed quite bizarre. But I think Father Schall was brilliantly defusing the silliness of the Boston Jesuit. I could not understand his reason in making a comparison between politicians and diapers - maybe partly joking and partly mocking Father Schall and I. But Father Schall brilliantly responded to his silliness philosophically.

We spent the rest of our kitchen table conversation by discussing random issues. Father Schall then invited me to have some dessert for our little celebration after we finished our dinner. Again, he congratulated me on my next mission to Notre Dame. He promised that he would give me a few names of his friends in Notre Dame that I could see. After we finished our dessert, Father Schall walked with me to my car, and I thanked him for his support and encouragement to pursue the intellectual apostolate. Then I said goodbye to Father Schall and drove back to Santa Clara.

The Eighteenth Saturday

On the Stupidity of an Education Degree

The month of May went by quickly, and I had been busy with my classes. June came, and we needed to get ready for the end of the Spring quarter, which marked the end of my journey at Santa Clara University. After graduation, we – the Jesuits in formation – must attend the National Formation Meeting in Loyola Marymount University in Los Angeles. In this gathering, all the Jesuits in training from the USA Jesuit Assistancy would get together in the same place. The theme of the meeting was *Global Mission in a Digital Age*.

I had been thinking of finding a time to visit Father Schall, but I had so many things to do and could not find a free Saturday to see him. Then, a Jesuit friend of mine, John Roselle, said that he would like to come to visit me before the formation gathering. We could drive together to Los Angeles for the national formation gathering. John said that he would also like to visit Father Schall if there was an opportunity to do so. The national formation gathering took place from June 15 -20; John would arrive on Saturday evening, June 13th, and head back to Milwaukee on the 21st. So our chance to visit Father Schall was only on Saturday, June 20th. I emailed Father Schall and told him that I was planning to visit him that Saturday. I explained to him that there was another fellow Jesuit from the Midwest Province who would come with me. We would drive back from Los Angeles in the morning and, hopefully, get to Los Gatos before dinner.

Father Schall said that he would be waiting for us for supper that evening.

After the long and tiring formation gathering in Los Angeles, John and I drove back to Northern California. We left early in the morning; the drive home went smoothly, and we got back to the South Bay around 4 PM, and still had plenty of time before the supper. I told John we should go straight to Los Gatos because I wanted to spend more time with Father Schall. But John had a crazy idea since he thought that we still had plenty of time. He wanted to buy a book by Father Schall and then get his signature. So we drove to a Catholic bookstore at Our Lady of Peace Church at Santa Clara. John decided to buy *The Order of Things*, partly because he believed it was a good book, and he wants to play a joke on our friend, Kevin Embach. He wanted to show to Kevin that he got Father Schall's signature on Kevin's favorite book.

We arrived in Los Gatos around 5 PM and checked in at the nursing station. I informed the nurse that we were Jesuits and Father Schall was expecting us. We went to Father Schall's room, and he let us in. Since there are only two chairs in the room, I sat on Father Schall's bed. Father Schall asked John about his background; he shared that he is originally from Oklahoma and then went to Creighton for undergraduate and majored in theology.

"Did you have a good education at Creighton?" Father Schall asked John.

"Oh yeah, Creighton is pretty orthodox compared to any other Jesuit Universities in the U.S."

Having known John for a little while, I knew that he had his own bias towards his alma mater. I said, "If you had a good education there, then why did you write a thesis that condemns Mother Teresa for simply practicing charity instead of justice?"

"I was just misguided at that time," said John.

Father jumped into the conversation and said, "Nothing is more confusing to students today than the difference between justice and charity, so no wonder you were misguided."

"We were bombarded with the notion of social justice, and I did not realize that I was just following the current."

"Yeah, many universities have become an arm of social justice. That's why it is important for students to learn proper philosophy so that they won't be misguided."

"Creighton still teaches philosophy, and we read classic authors," said John.

"The problem is the classic authors often contradict themselves. We must also have an education that recognizes that we can know the truth of things."

Father Schall paused for a moment and continued, "We, the American people, often think that we can learn everything. Everyone has a 'right' to a doctoral degree or even two doctorates. But having a Ph.D. these days does not mean you were trained in the love of wisdom. One can have a Ph.D. in Education, which is a preparation for someone to be a school administrator. It's stupid."

I knew that John had aspirations to have a Ph.D. degree in education, and I didn't know how he would react to Father Schall's statement. I decided to defuse the conversation by saying, "Oh yeah, by the way, Father Schall, John wants to have your inscription on one of your books. John, why don't you ask Father Schall to sign your book now?" John then showed the book to Father Schall, who immediately signed and wrote something on the title page.

"I really admire your dedication in writing books and articles. It's amazing that you are still publishing many books and articles in your retirement," said John.

"I have plenty of time in this place, and there is nothing else I can do besides writing."

"I hope that this man someday can follow your footstep," John pointed to me.

"I don't think anybody can replace Father Schall, but at least I have learned something from him on how we can build an intellectual life. I will be forever grateful for Sertillanges's book that you recommended."

"What is the book about?" asked John.

Father Schall explained about the book enthusiastically, "This is a book by a French Dominican who explains how you can build an intellectual life if you can keep up with the higher things of life for at least two hours a day. The book is primarily about discipline and how to rule oneself. You must read this book." He paused for a moment and asked, "What time is it now? I think it's time for us to go for supper."

Before we went to the dining room, Father Schall went to the restroom first. While waiting for Father Schall, John was trying to read the Father's Schall writing in the book, and he could not read it. After Father Schall came out of the restroom, John immediately asked:

"Sorry Father Schall, can you tell me what you wrote here?"

"My mom always said I am the only one who can read my own handwriting. It says, 'to John on the occasion of your visit to Los Gatos, California.'"

After Father Schall decrypted his handwriting, we moved to the dinning. Not long after we sat on the table and were enjoying our meals, John said something that I had been worrying about:

"Father Schall, although I was majoring in theology for my undergraduate, I have a master's degree in education. So I disagree with your opinion earlier about Ph.D. degrees in education."

Father Schall just smiled and said, "Do you have aspirations to be a university or high school president?"

"No, no, no, but I think that the science of education and the art of teaching is important. John Paul II said in his exhortation, *Catechesi Tradendae,* that pedagogy is one of the most important sciences."

"But JP II himself did not study how or why to study, but he studied what was worth knowing." Father Schall continued, "The author of *The Idea of a University* (John Henry Cardinal Newman) did not study education. Neither did St. Thomas Aquinas."

John Rosselle could be a combative person, and he often liked to fight. Before his exchange with Father Schall become heated, I decided to jump in and try again to defuse the conversation.

"By the way, John, why don't you share your project with Father Schall, and maybe he can give some advice."

John followed my suggestion by sharing his project on the virtue of heroism. He wanted to introduce the culture of heroism to his high school students and maybe spread it to many high school students and teenagers.

Father Schall recommended John read a dissertation titled *Aristotle on Heroes* that was directed by Ralph McInerny at the University of Notre Dame. John, himself, already made plans to attend a summer course for teachers at Notre Dame in the summer, so he was excited to look for the dissertation at the Notre Dame library. Father Schall then recommended John speak with one of the retired Jesuits who sat on the table across of us. He had taught at the Pontifical Biblical Institute (also known as "Biblicum") in Rome for many years. He recently came back to California for his retirement. Father Schall thought that Jesuit might have some insight about heroism from the biblical perspective.

While we were waiting for John to return from his conversation, Father Schall asked me about my preparations for my move to Notre Dame. I said that everything was already set, and I just needed to pack my stuff and hit the road. I would not leave until mid-August, so I should have plenty of time to see Father Schall.

After John finished his conversation, we said goodbye to Father Schall and drove back to Santa Clara. John spent a night at the Santa Clara Jesuit community, and then he left the following day back to Milwaukee. I was going to make my 8-day retreat in Barrington, Illinois in July. We planned to get together again in the Midwest in the coming month.

The Nineteenth Saturday

On the Classical Moment

A few days after John's departure, another Jesuit friend, Chris Grodecki from the Maryland Province, emailed me and said that he was planning to visit Santa Clara University Jesuit community, and he would like to visit Father Schall. Grodecki was at the same formation gathering at Loyola Marymount University. But he was taking a more extended break in Los Angeles before heading to Northern California. We planned to visit Father Schall on Saturday, June 27th.

I emailed Father Schall that I was planning to visit him for lunch, and there would be another Jesuit coming with me. Father Schall replied that he was looking forward to seeing us and asked me who the Jesuit coming with me was. I told Father Schall that this Jesuit fellow was Chris Grodecki, a Jesuit Scholastic from Maryland Province and a Georgetown alumnus. A little story of Chris Grodecki - he grew up in Winnetka, Illinois, in an affluent neighborhood, which was famous for the red brick, Georgian house, which 8-year-old Kevin McAllister defended in *Home Alone*. Grodecki was an incredibly talented piano player; he started playing piano when he was young and practiced diligently, which enabled him to play classical music brilliantly.

We came to the Sacred Heart Center around 11 AM, and after checking in at the nursing station, we went straight to Father Schall's room. I knocked on the door and heard the reply, "Come in." I opened the door and saw that Father Schall was reading the U.S. Supreme Court decision on *Obergefell v. Hodges*. The day before, the U.S. Supreme Court had issued the ruling that legalized same-sex marriage in the country. Father Schall printed the entire decision and read it carefully. I could see that he had highlighted and underlined many words from the decision.

Father Schall welcomed us to his small room, and as usual, I sat on his bed because there are only two chairs in his room. Chris Grodecki introduced himself as a Georgetown alumnus and a proud student of Father Schall.

"Sorry that I don't remember you in person because there were so many students in my classes. When did you study at Georgetown?" asked Father Schall.

"I was there from 2001 to 2005. I took your class on Elements of Political Theory," said Grodecki.

"Hmm, were you in the same class as the twin sisters?"

"I don't remember them. One thing that I remember about the class is that you required us to read an astounding twelve books."

Father Schall just smiled to hear Grodecki's comments. He then changed the subject by asking, "I heard that you are a classical pianist?"

Grodecki humbly replied, "I studied classical piano a little bit."

"It's good that you are interested in classical music," said Father Schall. He paused for a moment and asked us, "Have you heard the story of J.M. Coetzee and classical music?"

Unfortunately, neither of us had heard the story, and so Father Schall told it to us. "The young Coetzee one day heard some music from the house next door that he had never heard before. The music was Bach's 'Well-Tempered Clavier.' He froze as he listened to the music and felt that the music really spoke to him. This moment is what he called the Classic moment."

Father Schall then told us a story of how he taught courses on Plato and Aristotle for many years. But he was somewhat puzzled by the amount of space that music took up in the *Republic* and the *Politics*. It was not until he read the chapter on music in Allan Blooms' *The Closing of the American Mind* that he understood a change in music would signify a change in the polity. Father Schall explained further that we are formed by what we hear. Listening to music can affect our soul and it changes our whole mood. A disorder in music leads to a disorder of the soul. For this reason, Bloom said that the real educator of youth today is not the teacher but the music-makers.

"Keep playing your classical piano, and you can save many souls, "said Father Schall to Grodecki.

Grodecki just smiled.

"Did you major in Government at Georgetown?"

"No, I was majoring in English literature and German. I took your class because it was recommended as a course every student should take before leaving Georgetown."

"Oh, I thought you were majoring in Government and had a dream to go to law school like most of the undergraduates who major in Government."

"I did contemplate going to law school, and I worked at a non-profit public-interest law firm in D.C., but I decided to join the Novitiate."

"You made a better choice; otherwise, you will join the choirs of many lawyers who ruin the civilization as they did in yesterday's decision."

I have been quiet most of the time because I wanted to let Grodecki have a conversation with Father Schall. But I decided to jump into the discussion and asked, "Father Schall, what do you think about the Supreme Court's decision yesterday?"

"The Court decision is a betrayal of the nature of friendship," replied Father Schall. I was a bit surprised to hear Father Schall's statement. I was expecting him to say something along the lines of the betrayal of reason or natural law, but he raised the issue of friendship. I did not know what Grodecki thought about Father Schall's statement, so I decided to ask Father Schall to explain more.

Father Schall then began with an explanation of the classical Greek culture, where homosexual relations did exist. But neither Plato nor Aristotle approved these relations because of their view on friendship. They believed in a proper friendship between a man and his wife, a man and a man, a woman and a woman, and a man and a woman. The basis of the husband and wife friendship was home and children. This was a kind of friendship that required the two to live together for a lifetime. A man and a woman could have friendship with other men or women, but these were not marital friendships. More importantly, as Aristotle said, all friendships needed to be based on virtue and fidelity. For this reason, it is impossible to have a friendship without virtue, especially temperance.

Father Schall explained further that unless it was a marital situation, friendship is not sexual in any proper sense. This is the aspect of same-sex marriage that Justice Kennedy wanted to achieve: to make the relationship between same-sex couples proper. Father Schall believed that the primary reason behind Justice Kennedy's argument was marriage's legal bond, which would mitigate promiscuity. But in the end, the Court decision was a really a misunderstanding of the conditions of noble friendship and the basis for it to flourish.

I never thought about the relationship between *Obergefell* and friendship; again, Father Schall gave us a new insight into friendship. I switched the topic of discussion by saying, "I don't think you can blame all the lawyers for ruining civilization because there were still four judges who dissented."

"Indeed, those four justices issued vigorous dissents. The only way the five justices made this Court impose upon liberty was by simply not reading what their four colleagues had to say."

Father Schall paused for a moment and said, "What time is it now? I think it's time for us to have lunch."

We finished the conversation on that note and moved to the dining room. We did not have time for private discussion in the dining room because many of the retired Jesuits tried to speak with Grodecki, mainly because we sat on the big dining table with some other Jesuits. We had random conversation for the rest of the lunch. After lunch, we said goodbye to Father Schall; I told Father Schall that I had plans to travel to Hong Kong for a conference in early July, but I hoped to find a time to visit him soon. We then took off for the Santa Clara Jesuit villa in the Santa Cruz mountains.

The Twentieth Saturday

On *Gulliver's Travels* and a Super Bowl Ad

I was in Hong Kong in the first week of July for a conference at the University of Hong Kong. It was during the week of the 2015 FIFA Women's World Cup Finals, when the U.S. Women National Soccer Team won the World Cup. Santa Clara University was in euphoria over the Women's World Cup because their alumna, Julie Johnston, was on the U.S. Women's National Soccer Team. When I was in Hong Kong, I was thinking of emailing Father Schall and asking his opinion about the Women's World Cup. But although I knew that Father Schall as a sports fan, I guessed that women's soccer was not his forte. So I just emailed him and said that I planned to visit him after my return from Hong Kong.

I returned to the U.S. in the second week of July, hoping that I could spend more time with Father Schall during my next visit. In my last two trips, I had John Rosselle and Chris Grodecki with me, so I did not have any personal time with Father Schall. I was moving to Notre Dame in mid-August and would not have a lot of time with Father Schall after that. On top of that, I was to make my eight-day retreat in Illinois at the end of July. Practically, I only had two or three Saturdays to spend with Father Schall.

On that third Saturday of July, I was planning to visit Father Schall for supper, but in the morning, I received a phone call from a student who recently graduated from Santa Clara, named Lindsay Fay. Lindsay was a nice young lady who had a passion for all things pro-life, chastity related, and the new evangelization. She was the President of Broncos for Life, and in the last two years, I accompanied her in her journey as the pro-life leader on Santa Clara campus. In some ways, I considered Lindsay my mentee, and I wanted to continue to support her. Lindsay already had a plan to work as a missionary with the Culture Project. The Culture Project itself was a new enterprise when Lindsay decided to join the team. Cristina Barba, the founder of the Culture Project, launched the initiative in July 2014 with her vision to restore culture through the experience of virtue. Lindsay called me that morning and said that she was back in Santa Clara for the weekend and wanted to see me if I had time to meet.

On Saturday afternoon, I already planned to meet a former student from the Law School and her husband. In the evening, I was expecting to see Father Schall for supper. Lindsay was busy on Sunday because she planned to visit some parishes in the area to fundraise for her missionary works. Finally, I suggested to Lindsay that she join me in my visit to Father Schall. We could discuss things on the car ride to Los Gatos.

We drove to Los Gatos, and as we were approaching the Sacred Heart Center property, we saw a young deer running across the street. I don't know how many deer lived there, but it's common to see them on the one hundred-eighty acre property of the Sacred Heart Jesuit Center. Lindsay was so excited to see the deer and thought it was a good omen for her at the start of her missionary journey.

When we checked in the nursing station, I asked the nurse to call Father Schall because I didn't want to bring Lindsay to his room.

The nurse called Father Schall's room and let me speak with him; I informed Father Schall that I couldn't come to his room because I had a female guest. Father Schall then told me to meet him in front of the dining room. It was close to supper time anyway, so it was better for us to start supper.

I introduced Lindsay to Father Schall as a recent Santa Clara alumna. She was about to start her missionary project serving college students and young people.

"Are you going to work with Focus?" asked Father Schall.

"No, I am going to work with the Cultural Project."

"I never heard about it."

"It's a new organization, and some of the leaders used to work for Focus."

"Where is home for you?"

"Southern California, Orange County."

We grabbed some food for our supper and sat at a private table. Father Schall then asked Lindsay, "Do you want to have a glass of wine?"

"Yes, please."

"You sit there; I will get it for you."

"Father Schall, I have been visiting you for many months, but you never offered me a glass of wine. Now you offer this beautiful young lady a glass of wine," I said jokingly.

"I am not worried about you because I know that you can take care of yourself," Father Schall replied with a smile.

We began to enjoy our meal and Father Schall asked Lindsay, "What are you going to do with this Cultural Project?"

"We will live in a parish and try to reach out to young people, either in the parishes or in Catholic high schools. We will try to open a discussion with them about the meaning of real love, chastity, and sexual integrity."

"Have you ever read Jonathan Swift's letter to Alexander Pope?"

"No."

"Do you know who Jonathan Swift is?"

"No."

"He was an Irish writer and poet. One of his famous works was *Gulliver's Travels*. Sorry for asking these questions, but I don't know what kind of classic English literature you read in Santa Clara."

One of the greatest lessons I learned by knowing Father Schall was that of humility. One needed humility to admit how much we don't know when having a conversation with Father Schall. But I didn't know how Lindsay was going to take being reminded how much she didn't know. I interjected the conversation by saying, "I watched the cartoon of *Gulliver's Travels* when I was young, but I had no clue about Jonathan Swift."

"It's amazing that *Gulliver's Travels* is well known in Indonesia," said Father Schall.

"Well, I just knew it through a cartoon movie. So, Father Schall, what's the story of Jonathan Swift?"

"In his letter to Alexander Pope, Swift argued that we could not properly love an abstraction. He wrote that the problem of the people of the twentieth century was that they tried to love abstractions. The object our real loves are not abstractions. You should keep this mind when you talk about real love next year."

Lindsay was a smart young lady, but her Santa Clara education may not have equipped her to discuss an abstract moral theological concept. I was afraid that the conversation would end up as a deep philosophical and theological discussion. I tried to switch the conversation to a different topic.

"Father Schall, you are a big fan of Super Bowl, right? Lindsay has a story that you might like to hear about one of the Super Bowl ads this year."

"What's the story?" said Father Schall with excitement.

Lindsay knew what I meant, so she began to share the story of her dad who was the brain behind the Toyota Super Bowl 2015 ad, titled 'My Bold Dad.' Lindsay's dad worked for Toyota. He was involved in proposing a new idea for the 2015 Toyota Super Bowl ad. The rhetoric of the ad and the storyline presented had something to do with the softer side of fatherhood and how men embrace that role. Lindsay explained that several sequences were worth recalling; the main sequence showed the dad dropping his daughter off for military deployment.

In a flashback, the ad shows that when she was a little girl, the dad chose to do various things like capture spiders and eradicate beehives from tree houses. The dad stood up for his little girl against a bully. The ad also showed some sequences of the dad's relationship with his adult daughter. He asked her daughter to dance when nobody wanted to dance with her. The dad picked the daughter up from a party that had gone wrong. The final sequence of the ad shows the dad dropping his daughter off at the airport and watching, with tears in his eyes, as his daughter goes off to join the military as an adult.

After hearing Lindsay's story, Father Schall responded, "Sounds like a good ad. I missed it because I did not want to watch the Superbowl ads, many of which are full of political propaganda."

I am a bit curious about what kind of propaganda Father Schall meant, so I asked him, "What kind of propaganda do you think are in those ads?"

"If you pay attention, in recent years, some of the ads contain a heavy dose of propaganda about equality. But the ad that her dad made seems immune from that propaganda."

"I can send the video to you later if you like," I told Father Schall.

"Yes, please send it to me."

We spend the rest of the dinner discussing random issues, but at the end of our dinner, Father Schall asked a question of Lindsay, "Do you have a beau? A nice young lady like you must have a beau."

"Yes," said Lindsay.

"Is he a missionary like you?"

"No, he is an engineer."

"Two of you met in Santa Clara?"

"No, he went to Louisiana State. We met at a Theology of the Body Summer internship in Philadelphia."

"Good for you that you have met and fallen in love with what seems to be a great guy!"

We finished our supper, and before we left, Father Schall introduced Lindsay to Father John Privett, the Superior of the Sacred Heart Center, who was also originally from Southern California. They had a little conversation about Southern California, and then we said goodbye to Father Schall. I was a bit surprised to see Father

Schall give a kiss on the cheek to Linday. But I guess it was a gesture to show his respect to her.

I told Father Schall that I would be away for my 8-day retreat in Illinois. Hopefully I would have time to see him in August before my departure to Notre Dame. We drove back to Santa Clara and I said goodbye to Lindsay and wished her all the best on her missionary journey.

Back home, I pulled up the video of the ad we'd talked about and sent it to Father Schall. Then I watched it again; the narration from the ad said: "Being a dad is more than being a father, it's a choice. A choice to get hurt rather than to hurt. To be bold when others are scared. A choice that says that you will be there. To show them right or wrong. By your words and your actions. Being a dad is more than being a father; it's a commitment, one that will make a wonderful human being, who will make their own choices."

I will never be a dad, but I hope that I can be a good spiritual father for many. A spiritual father who can show my spiritual sons and daughters right from wrong, with my words and actions. I am committed to being a spiritual father for many, and I hope that they will find the place where they meant to be and to cooperate with God's plan for them.

The Twenty-First Saturday

On the Way to Notre Dame

I wished I could have spent more time with Father Schall, but I had to leave for my annual 8 day retreat in Barrington, Illinois. I have been making a retreat to this place for two years in a row, but Barrington was not my favorite place. It happened that the retreat program for Jesuits in training always takes place there. A year before, I was doing a retreat with some fellow Jesuit regents in Barrington. Now, the Jesuits Constitution retreat was in the same place.

I came home from the retreat on the feast of St. Ignatius of Loyola on July 31st. I was planning to leave for Notre Dame on August 15th. I emailed Father Schall and said I expected to see him for the last time on August 8th. We planned to meet for lunch, but I came a bit early as I was hoping to spend more time with Father Schall. After checking in the nursing station, I went to his room, and he let me sit on the chair.

Surprisingly, Father Schall chose to spend our conversation by recommending me a lot of books to read. First, he recommended me to read *Seeing Things Politically: Interviews with Benedicte Delorme-Montini,* by Pierre Manent. I had no idea who Pierre Mannet was. Father Schall then told me that Mannet was a French political scientist and academic. Father Schall recommended me to check out Mannet's earlier books, *Tocqueville and the Nature of Democracy* and *The City of Man.*

While I was still busy digesting information about Pierre Mannet, Father Schall showed me another book titled *Icarus Fallen: The Search for Meaning in an Uncertain World,* by Chantal Delsol. Again, I had no clue who Chantal Delsol is. It turned out that she was a French philosopher, political historian, and novelist. Father Schall recommended I read the sequel of the book, titled *The Unlearned Lessons of the Twentieth Century: An Essay On Late Modernity,* and the final installment of the trilogy, titled *Unjust Justice: Against the Tyranny of International Law.*

"Have you read Catherine Pickstock's *After Writing*?"

"No, and I have no idea who she is."

"She is a philosopher-theologian from Cambridge; you must have read her book?"

"What's special about her book?"

"You will be ordained as a priest in a few years, so you must take liturgy seriously. This remarkable book will help you to understand the nature of the classic Roman liturgy."

"So this book is about liturgy?"

"Not really, it is more a contemplation of philosophy through a kind of liturgy."

"Sounds interesting! I will check out this book."

Father Schall did not stop with *After Writing*; he recommended me to check out other publications of Pickstock. It turned out that Pickstock was the co-founder of the *Radical Orthodoxy* movement along with John Millbank. I heard about John Millbank a bit during my philosophy study in Chicago, but I never heard about *Radical Orthodoxy* until Father Schall told me.

"Do you who Remi Brague is?"

"If I am not mistaken, he is a French philosopher-theologian. I heard his name as one of the recipients of the Ratzinger Prize."

In 2012, Brague received the Ratzinger prize. The other recipient was a Jesuit, Father Brian Daley from Notre Dame. I met Brian Daley for a couple of times, and I had been in contact with him as I transitioned to Notre Dame for the coming academic year. When I came to visit the Jesuit house in Notre Dame, I saw a picture of Brian Daley, Remi Brague, and Pope Benedict XVI.

"Have you ever read his books?" asked Father Schall.

"No."

"I highly recommend you read his book, *The Legend of the Middle Ages*." Of course, Father Schall did not stop there; he recommended me to check out Brague's other books, such as *On the God of the Christians*, *The Law of God*, and *Eccentric Culture*.

Finally, Father Schall showed me his newly published book, *On Christians and Prosperity*.

"I don't have an extra copy, otherwise, I would give you one. But you can order this book easily from the publisher."

I felt a kind of weird because Father Schall was dumping so many books recommendation on me. Maybe he knew that he might not see me again for a long time. I hoped to see Father Schall from time to time during my visits back in California. But Father Schall turned 87 years old; we did not know how long he might live here on earth.

"What time is now?" asked Father Schall.

"It's about ten past noon."

"Let's go for lunch."

We moved to the dining room for our lunch. We sat at the same table with other Jesuit and did not have a private conversation. Two nights before, the first Republican Party debate occurred at the Quicken Loans Arena in Cleveland, Ohio. Our kitchen table conversation soon began to revolve around the discussion. It was Fox News that hosted the debate and one of the Jesuits at our table said,

"I never watch Fox News, and I don't know what's appealing about that station."

Surprisingly, Father Schall jumped into the conversation and commented, "If you never watch the Fox News, of course, you won't know anything appealing about that station."

"So tell me, Jim, what is appealing from Fox News?"

"If you watch the station, you will see that they have many blonde lawyers with long legs."

I was a bit surprised to hear Father Schall's comment. I didn't know who he was referring to, whether it was Megyn Kelly, the Fox News star anchor or someone else. I was not sure if Father Schall watched Fox News because of those blonde lawyers. Maybe he was just playing with his fellow Jesuits.

We spent the rest of our time conversing on random issues. After lunch, Father Schall walked with me to my car. I decided to ask him a blunt question, "Well, Father Schall, I do not know when we will be able to meet again; do you have any last words for me?"

He replied, "My generation has been provided with the education and opportunities to live a life relatively free to read and write. The leisure to wonder about what it is all about has been a great gift to me from the Society of Jesus."

He paused for a moment and continued, "I hope that your generation still has such an opportunity. Treasure your next year in Notre Dame with your writing and reading."

It was surprising but not shocking to hear Father Schall share his wisdom about reading and writing.

Father Schall continued, "Don't waste your time with unimportant stuff. You are not old, but you are not young either, so you don't have a lot of time left in your intellectual journey."

As I was driving my car out of the parking lot, Father Schall stood in front of the Sacred Heart Center and waved his hand. I didn't know when I would see him again, but I knew I had been blessed to get to know Father Schall in the last two years of my regency in Santa Clara.

Sojourn at Notre Dame I

On Writing, Reading, Praying, and Playing

I arrived at the University of Notre Dame on the feast of the Assumption of the Blessed Mother, August 15, 2015. It was a blessing for me to come to Our Lady's University on her feast day. My Jesuit friend, John Roselle, picked me at the airport and drove me to Notre Dame. John said that it was his heroic journey to drive from Milwaukee, where he lived, pick me up at Midway airport, and drive to Notre Dame.

After stopping for dinner at a local Chinese restaurant in South Bend, we arrived at Henri de Lubac House Jesuit Community at around 9 PM. After unloading our luggage, we walked to the Grotto and prayed for the intercession of Our Lady. On the following day, John drove back to Milwaukee, and I began my sojourn at Notre Dame.

On the surface, my daily activity was dull as I spent my time mostly writing and reading. But I enjoyed the leisure – as Father Schall liked to say - that I had for reading and writing. I had the leisure to read and write during my doctoral studies at the University of Washington. But at that time, I was too focused on my dissertation project, which was on the judicial review process in a new democracy, especially of the experience of my home country, Indonesia. Hence, my readings and writings were very narrow, and I did not have time to read many philosophical or theological books. Plus, at that time, I was just a naïve Ph.D. student who did not know what to read outside my narrow field of study.

I came to Notre Dame intending to turn my dissertation into a book. With six years of Jesuit training, I thought that I was already a better person than I was during my years as a graduate student when I wrote my dissertation. I was planning to use the Aristotelian notion of heroism and his virtue theory as the theoretical framework for my book. I read a lot of Aristotle and classical Greek literature. One of the primary scholarly imaginations in constitutional theory is Homer's *Odyssey*. Jon Elster successfully created tremendous interest in the notion of constitutions as exercises of self-binding – referring to a metaphor of Odysseus having himself bound to the mast to hear the Sirens safely.

In my book project, I was trying to provide a new narrative on the heroism of Odysseus. Consequently, I read a lot of commentary on Homer's *Odyssey*. Once, I asked a favor from my Jesuit Superior, Father Michael Magree, S.J., to return some books to the Hesburgh Library. At that time, I was away on Christmas break in Santa Clara, so I asked Father Magree to come to my room and return some interlibrary loan books. Father Magree, who studied Classics at the University of Steubenville, was surprised to see that I had so many books about the Odyssey.

Father Schall had often considered the years he spent in philosophical studies at Mount St. Michael's in Spokane to be the most interesting and formative ones of his many years of clerical and academic studies. Father Schall could quickly point to his years at St. Michael as the best years in his Jesuit formation because he had superb instructors at St. Michael. I had some superb instructors in my philosophy studies, but my overall philosophy education was far below the quality of education that Father Schall received at Mount St. Michael. I don't think that I could consider my philosophy studies in Loyola Chicago as the best formative years in my Jesuit education. Nevertheless, I liked to consider my time in Notre Dame as one of the most exciting times in my Jesuit clerical and academic studies, mainly because I had a good deal of time that allowed for the leisure to think and write.

There is a famous saying, "publish or perish"; I was trying hard to publish my book so that I would not perish. But publishing a book is not an easy thing to do, and I had to deal with rejections from publishers. In many moments of disappointment and desperation, I had nowhere to go but to turn to the Blessed Mother and asked her intercession to help me find a publisher.

A few years ago, when I did my interview at Santa Clara University for my regency assignment, I had an exciting encounter with a Jesuit Brother named Tom Brakow. Tom Brakow is a humble man, and his job was an assistant to the Father Minister at Santa Clara Jesuit community. On that evening, within the ten minutes' drive to the San Jose airport, he gave me the best advice that I ever received on the Jesuit life. He said that there are three things that you must do to be a good Jesuit, "be a man of prayer, trust God in everything, and always turn to the Blessed Mother for help."

During my sojourn at Notre Dame, I had no other choice than to be a man of prayer, trusting God in my book project, and asking the intercession of the Blessed Mother to help me. Apart from the book project, I also had to rely on God for many different things, such as my immigration status. At that time, I had been residing in the United States for over ten years. But because of stupid reasons with the immigration lawyer that handled my case, I did not have permanent residency yet. I had been given many different immigration statuses, from a religious worker, a student, a temporary worker, and back again to a religious worker. I had some trouble getting a new religious worker status when I arrived at Notre Dame, which almost jeopardized my appointment. It was only through the intercession of the Blessed Mother that I finally got the new immigration status.

Finally, after Notre Dame, I had to move to theological studies, a final stage in the Jesuit formation before Ordination. I had to be approved for theological studies. Again, I prayed mightily that the Society of Jesus would approve me for advancing to theological studies and moving toward priestly Ordination. My friend John Roselle made an analogy of the process of applying to theology as a political campaign. But I respectfully disagree with his analogy of a campaign. I think that this application process was a time that I should trust in God's Providence as to whether He considered me worthy to be His priest. Of course, in no way was I worthy of being a priest because I am a sinner like all others. But at least I must have faith that despite all my shortcomings, God had chosen me to be one of His servants.

During his long pilgrimage, St. Ignatius of Loyola always made a constant petition to the Blessed Mother "that she would place him with her Son." During my sojourn in Notre Dame, I also made a constant petition to the Blessed Mother; I often went to the Grotto and begged the Blessed Mother that she would place me with her Son, leading me to be a priest in the least of the Society of Jesus.

Apart from reading, writing, and praying, I experienced one important aspect of life at Notre Dame, playing. The playing aspect was partly related to the football culture in Notre Dame. I did not know about American football until I came to the United States, but I did not come to know more about the rules of football and enjoy watching the game until I came to Notre Dame. In my email correspondence with Father Schall, he encouraged me to use the opportunity to enjoy football games while I was at Notre Dame.

I initially resisted Father Schall's recommendation because I thought that a Catholic university like Notre Dame should invest more in their educational infra-structure instead of football. But Father Schall convinced me that a real civilization could not exist without certain play elements. He then recommended me to read a book titled *Homo Ludens*, which means men who play games, written by a Dutch historian and cultural theorist, Johan Huizinga. Father Schall argued that I should not consider watching a good football game as wasting my time because in watching a game, we adhere to a kind of wonder about something that takes place before us, even if only for a brief moment.

Thanks to the generosity of a few members of Congregation of the Holy Cross (CSC), we, the Jesuits, received some free tickets to the football game. With the CSC tickets, I could enjoy many football games, and some were good seat tickets. The Notre Dame team started their regular season with a blowout game against the Texas Longhorns, by a score of 38-3. They seemed on the path to creating history when they had another blowout game, with a score of 62- 27 against UMass. But then they ended the season with two consecutive losses, first 36-38 defeat against Stanford for the Legends Trophy, and finally, the Irish were defeated by Ohio State in the Fiesta Bowl by a score of 44–28. There was nothing special for the Notre Dame fans in the 2015 season, but it was a new beginning for me as an Irish fan.

Apart from enjoying football, I had another important lesson of enjoying life from my time at Notre Dame. During my sojourn, I got to know a beautiful Catholic young lady, originally from Argentina, named Clara Minieri. Clara was a woman who some would call a "perfect package." She was beautiful, had an excellent personality, was highly intelligent, and was also a devout Catholic. At that time, she was pursuing her Master of Law degree (LLM) at the Notre Dame Law School. One important lesson that Clara taught me was how to celebrate and to enjoy life. During Catholic feast days, for instance, like the Feast of Immaculate Conception, Clara brought some chocolate and donuts and offered it to all of us after Mass. "This is the feast day of Our Lady and so we must celebrate," said Clara. On every major feast day in the Roman Catholic calendar, you could expect Clara to be ready with chocolate or different kinds of sweets in front of St. Thomas More Chapel at Notre Dame Law School.

My birthday was April 13, which usually comes around Easter time, and it also came close to the end of the semester when I was busy with work, and everybody was too busy to join me for a celebration of my life. I usually do not bother to celebrate; but during my sojourn at Notre Dame, Clara decided to throw a small party for me. She said that we should celebrate even if it was only a tiny celebration amid our busy work.

Perhaps one of the biggest challenges in our lives is receiving love because often, we feel unworthy to receive such love. With all of the unresolved emotional attachments in my life, I had some difficulty in receiving love; when I was a graduate student in Seattle, I rejected a surprise party from my housemates because I had trouble accepting their love. But at Notre Dame, I let Clara organize a small birthday party because I knew that she loved and cared for me as a friend. Indeed, my sojourn in Notre Dame was one of the most exciting times in my Jesuit clerical formation.

Sojourn at Notre Dame II

Friends of Father Schall

During my sojourn in Notre Dame, Ignatius Press re-issued *The Wiseman from the West*, Vincent Cronin's 1955 biography of a great Jesuit missionary, Matteo Ricci, S.J. (1552-1610). Father Schall recommended that I read the book; not only was it an important book about a great Jesuit missionary, but also it contains Ricci's reflection on the centrality and importance of friendship.

When I was a Jesuit novice, I spent a little time learning about Jesuit history in China. At that time, I resided three months at the University of San Francisco. I studied Jesuit history in China under the tutelage of Father Antoni Urceler, S.J., a Jesuit scholar at the Ricci Institute at the University of San Francisco. I did remember that Ricci wrote a treatise, *On Friendship: One Hundred Maxims for a Chinese Prince*. He wrote the treatise with the hope that the Chinese could see that friendship was also alive in the Western tradition. Here Ricci tried to build a dialogue on classical Western writers such as Cicero, Aristotle, and Confucius' thoughts on friendship.

One especially interesting aspect of the Chinese discussion was how many friends one could have. Aristotle had said that a "friend of everybody is a friend of nobody." But unlike Aristotle, during his time in China, Ricci strived to make many friends among the Chinese. In one of his maxims, Ricci wrote, "when Wo-Mo Pi (a renowned ancient scholar) cut open a large pomegranate, someone asked him: 'Master, what things would you like to have as numerously as these seeds?' To which he responded: 'Fruitful friends.'"[33] Indeed, during his time in China, he made so many friends that his friendships often became rather time-consuming. In his letter to his brother, Anton Maria Ricci, dated in late August 1608, less than two years before his death, Ricci wrote:

"I have friends everywhere, so many that they will not let me live, and I spend the whole day in the living rooms answering different questions, apart from the task that I have here."[34]

Father Schall seemed skeptical of Ricci's conviction on having many friends. He tended to follow Aristotle in that one cannot have many friends at the same time. The only possible way for us to have many friends at the same time is through the idea of eternal life where we can be friends with many after in the afterlife. But during my sojourn at Notre Dame, I met many people who considered themselves friends of Father Schall.

One day I met Bruce Fingerhut, the director of St. Augustine Press, at a conference at Notre Dame. St. Augustine Press published many books of Father Schall's. I asked him why his company had invested so much in publishing Father Schall's books. He answered

---

[33] Matteo Ricci, translated by Timothy Billings, *On Friendship: One Hundred Maxims for a Chinese Prince* (Columbia University Press; Bilingual edition, September 17, 2009), Maxims # 100, p. 137.

[34] Pietro Tacchi Venturi S.J., *Opere Storiche del P. Matteo Ricci S.I. Comitato per le onoranze nazionali con prolegomena* (Macerata: Giorgetti, 1911–1913), 2 vols; II, 376.

that Father Schall was a C.S. Lewis for our time. While I was not sure that Father Schall would consider himself another C.S. Lewis, Fingerhut was immensely proud to be a friend of the C.S. Lewis of our time. Through their collaboration in publishing books, Fingerhut considered Father Schall as his good friend.

Then there was Patrick Deenen, a professor of Political Science at the University of Notre Dame. Deenen used to teach in the Government Department at Georgetown University. Deenen was a colleague of Father Schall at Georgetown. In 2012, the same year that Father Schall retired from Georgetown, Deenen left Georgetown to accept a new post at Notre Dame.

One day, I sat with Deenen at Notre Dame and discussed many different things; one of the topics we discussed was Father Schall. Deenen praised Father Schall as an exceptionally gifted teacher; in Deenen's estimation in one academic year, Father Schall might have taught around 500 students at Georgetown. This calculation was based on the fact that Father Schall taught several big classes. The bottom line was that Deenen believed Father Schall was a magnet for students at Georgetown, and he had a great impact on those young men and women.

I also met a Georgetown alumna named Cindy Searcy at the Notre Dame Vita Institute, an intensive intellectual formation program for leaders in the national and international pro-life movement. Cindy herself was a student of Father Schall at Georgetown. She grew up in the Presbyterian tradition and converted to Catholicism during her time in Georgetown, especially after getting to know Father Schall. After her graduation, she continued to be friends with Father Schall. Father Schall once said that when a class walked out the door on the last day, the chances were slim that a teacher would ever see 95 percent of the students again.[35] Cindy fell into the category of that 5 percent of students who regularly saw Father Schall and formed a friendship with him over the years.

Apart from meeting Cindy at the Vita Institute, I met a young man named Christian (not his real name) who shared an exciting story about his interaction with Father Schall. This fellow had been accepted to medical school and was about to begin his medical studies in the following Fall semester. When his sister wanted to give him a gift for graduation, he asked his sister for a ticket to California to see Father Schall. So as a graduation gift, he got a chance to meet Father Schall in Los Gatos. It was amazing that this young man chose to see Father Schall as his graduation gift instead of many other gifts that he could have enjoyed. When I asked this fellow why he wanted to see Father Schall, he said that he had long admired Father Schall through his writings.

Indeed, Father Schall had such a huge impact on many young men and women through his writings. Reading his essays or books is like wrapping your mind in a time-traveling tapestry of transcendent themes and truths — where classical philosophy, history, theology, politics, music, sports, culture, and Charlie Brown are all interwoven.

In reflecting on the many people that I met in Notre Dame who knew Father Schall, I was not sure if one could say that Father Schall

---

[35] Kathryn Jean Lopez, "A Living University: A Conversation with Rev. James V. Schall," *Catholic Education Resource Center*, https://www.catholiceducation.org/en/education/catholic-contributions/a-living-university-a-conversation-with-rev-james-v-schall.html

had many friends. I don't know if Father Schall would consider all of them his friends in the first place. Some of them were more fans or admirers than friends. If Father Schall wanted to follow Ricci's maxim of friendship, he might call all of them his friends. But in the Aristotelian sense, maybe only one or two of them were truly Father Schall's friends.

Moreover, I began to wonder about my relationship with Father Schall. I didn't know whether Father Schall considered me a friend or merely a naïve Jesuit Scholastic, trying to find a father figure. I thought I would ask this question directly to Father Schall when I next had a chance to see him again in Los Gatos.

The Twenty-Second Saturday

On Aristotle and Publishing a Book

During my sojourn at Notre Dame, I had been corresponding via email regularly with Father Schall. But I missed face to face meetings with him. During a Christmas break, I went back to Santa Clara hoping to see Father Schall. But it turned out that he already had planned to spend Christmas vacation with his niece in Los Angeles. It was not until June 2016 that I finally had a chance to see Father Schall again.

Every year, all of the Jesuits in training must get together for an annual "summer camp" at a Jesuit retreat house in Applegate, Northern California. The summer camp was followed by a big gathering for the priestly Ordination. In 2016, the Ordination was to take place in Spokane, Washington. But I decided to leave the summer camp earlier so that I could visit Father Schall before flying to Spokane.

On the first Saturday of the month, June 4, 2016, I finally met Father Schall again at the Sacred Heart Jesuit Center in Los Gatos. As usual, Father Schall was sitting in front of the computer and writing something when I came to his room. I could not describe how excited I was to finally see Father Schall again. I started the conversation by asking Father Schall about his health; he seemed to be doing fine for an 88-year-old man. Father Schall then asked me about

living in Notre Dame. Soon the conversation evolved to a more serious discussion; it began with Father Schall asking me to share
about my research project.

I told Father Schall that I was trying to challenge the prevailing
fascination of both American and international constitutional law
scholars with the siren song story in Homer's *Odyssey*. It was a Nor-
wegian political theorist named Jon Elster who posits the notion of
constitutions as exercises of self-binding – referring to a metaphor
of Odysseus having himself bound to the mast to hear the sirens
safely. Elster specifically refers to Odysseus, who is unwilling to
forgo the opportunity to listen to the sirens' song. Therefore, he in-
structs his crew to tie him to the mast of the boat before they meet
the sirens. He also gave his crew beeswax to plug their ears and told
them further to lash him more tightly to the mast if he protested.

This metaphor has been cited many times by constitutional
scholars around the world. But I think that those constitutional theorists have missed seeing the real Odysseus himself. Most of the constitutional scholars these days are the children or the grandchildren
of the Warren Court, so they see the rule of a judge as a hero who
must correct many perceived social wrongs. Thus, their understanding of heroism is based on the understanding that if the hero found
someone who blocked his path, he would fight against the obstacle
until something broke. But the real Odysseus is an atypical hero; instead of battering his head against the obstacle, he will find un-seem-
ingly heroic ways to achieve his goal. For example, he faced Polyphemus, a vicious one-eyed giant known as a Cyclops, who trapped
Odysseus and his men in a cave. A typical Greek hero would have

chosen to kill Polyphemus, but Odysseus decides to trick the Cyclops by claiming that his name was "Nobody" and leaving the cave hanging onto a ram's belly.

To address this issue, I turned to the Aristotelian's notion of heroism. Aristotle elaborates on the hero's concept in *Nicomachean Ethics*, in which he discusses the first two virtues: *andreia* (courage or manliness) and *sophrosune* (temperance). For Aristotle, heroism must, therefore, be discussed concerning courage and temperance. Here Aristotle makes a classical comparison between two characters of Homeric heroes: Achilles of *Iliad* and Odysseus of *Odyssey*. Achilles is the exemplar of *andreia* and Odysseus is of *sophrosune*, and Aristotle praises them both because they embody different models of heroic virtue.

After hearing my explanation, Father Schall asked, "Have you heard of a new book, *Aristotelian Interpretation* by Fran O'Rourke?"

"No."

"You should read the book because it will be helpful for your research."

"Does the author discuss the idea of heroism?"

"Not specifically, but he refers to James Joyce' *Ulysses*. Have you read Joyce's *Ulysses*?"

"I came across Joyce a lot in my research, but I did not read him because I thought he was just a novelist."

"It's more than a novel; you must read it because Joyce was brilliantly using an analogy in the book, which he gained from his study of Aristotle. Your research is about analogies, right? So you will learn something from Joyce's brilliant analogy."

"Okay, Father Schall, now you gave me homework to read two books: first the book on Aristotle that you recommended and second, James Joyce' *Ulysses*."

Father Schall just smiled and said, "You have the whole summer to read the books, so it's doable."

"Well, I still have to work on my manuscript this summer. I am hoping to finish the manuscript before I go into theology."

A few months before, I received the good news that the Society of Jesus had approved my advancement in theological studies. My time at Notre Dame was coming to an end. I would move to Boston at the end of summer and start my theological studies at Boston College School of Theology and Ministry.

Father Schall then asked me, "Do you already have a contract for your book?"

"No. Father Schall, that is something that I want to ask you about. You published many books in your lifetime. Do you have any tips on how to secure a book contract? I have been trying to secure a book contract for the last year and have had zero results."

"Tell me more about your story to find a publisher."

I began to share my struggles in finding a publisher. First, I tried to send my proposal to Cambridge University Press, and then they send my proposal for external review. Both reviewers came back with negative results, and so Cambridge rejected my proposal. Then I tried to send my proposals to many publishers; most of them either never got back to me or rejected me right away. Then I found a possibility at Hart Publishing in England, but again, the external reviewers were not very favorable. Reviewer A wanted me to add three new chapters, and Reviewer B merely rejected my proposal. The editor then concluded that my book was not worthy of publication. Now I was looking for a new publisher, and at the same time, I had been working on revising my manuscript by adding the three new chapters.

After hearing my sorrow, Father Schall replied, "Don't give up. Keep trying to submit your proposal. Look up their procedures and send it in. Otherwise, you waste time. You know that publishers have millions of manuscripts. So you need to be prepared to have many papers of rejection in your drawer."

"A few years ago, I watched an Israeli drama film titled *Footnote*. The main character in the movie is a scholar who never published anything significant in his career. His only claim to fame was being mentioned in a footnote in the work of a more famous scholar. I hope that I won't be like that man."

"Well, you know that western philosophical tradition consists of a series of footnotes to Plato and Aristotle. And Christian theology is a series of footnotes to Augustine and Aquinas. In some way or another, all work will be a footnote."

Father Schall continued, "Keep trying to finish your manuscript and publish it, but it was not unusual that a good scholar might spend his whole life writing a book or two that only four or five people in the world could understand or read."

Here again, more wisdom from Father Schall. He was a great scholar who produced a lot, but he remained humble, and now he reminded me that I should not be dreaming that my book would become a best seller. Maybe my book would just end up in a dark corner of a library and only a handful of people would read it.

Father Schall continued, "A book is a mystery because you never really know who will read it and how it may influence other people. Christopher Morley once said that books are like explosives that just sit there waiting to go off."

I responded, "Huh...many years ago, I bought a book written by Archbishop Chaput from a used bookstore in Seattle. It was a slender book, titled *Living Catholic Faith*. The book was pretty instrumental in my vocation to the priesthood, especially after I read what Archbishop Chaput wrote, that without a priest, there would be no Eucharist, and without the Eucharist, there would be no Church."

"You see, a book is really like an explosive," said Father Schall.

We finished our conversation, then we moved to the dining room and had lunch. During lunch, Father Schall proudly introduced me to some other Jesuits as a Jesuit Scholastic who was about to start my theological studies at Boston College in the fall. Here we go again! Father Schall played the fatherly figure who proudly introduced his spiritual son to others. As I rarely received many compliments from my biological father, I treasured my spiritual father's pride in me. Indeed, Father Schall was a father figure to me in many ways. That day, he encouraged me to work on my manuscript and find a publisher. But at the same time, he also reminded me that realistically, my book might just end up on a dusty shelf in a library.

After lunch, I said goodbye to Father Schall; I told him that I wished to spend the summer in California, but I needed to go back to Notre Dame and work on my manuscript. I did not think I would have a chance to work on the manuscript after I started my theological studies in the fall. Father Schall then reminded me that theological studies were particularly important because they were the final preparation for my priestly Ordination. So even if I could not finish my manuscript or find a publisher, there was something bigger waiting for me, that is, the path to the priesthood.

The Twenty-Third Saturday

On Aquinas, Scalia, and Losing Sports Teams

I could not finish the manuscript by the end of summer, but I moved to Boston to start my theological studies. Not long after I left Notre Dame, Archbishop Charles Chaput gave a lecture at Notre Dame titled, *Things Worth Dying For: The Nature of a Life Worth Living.* Interestingly, Father Schall wrote me an email:

"Did you see the Chaput talk at Notre Dame, the world's losing football team?"

I wrote back to Father Schall: "I had already left Notre Dame when Chaput came to give a talk. But I read the transcript of his speech, which was a fantastic speech. Notre Dame is losing in their football games, perhaps because the Blessed Mother is taking away Her blessings after ND gave the Latare Medal to Joe Biden. This statement might be sound superstitious, but I think Notre Dame will have to live with its sin of awarding Biden the Latare Medal."

Father Schall immediately replied to my email: "You are an old testament Prophet; God punished the Israelites for being diso-bedient. ND is a Pope Francis Christian, all is mercy, so they should begin to win soon."

Finally, Father Schall wrote, "I do not think the BC grid team is doing much either, so they are probably being punished for a similar delict!"

Well, it was just a playful email exchange between us. In the 2015 season, Boston College became the first to go winless in football and basketball in 40 years. The football team went 0-8 in the ACC play in 2015, and then their basketball team fell to 0-18 in the ACC play.

I was new at Boston College, so I did not have any allegiance to BC, and so I didn't care about BC's losing season. But I remembered that once Father Schall said that revelation had been designed with losers in mind.[36] Revelation is filled with words like salvation, repentance, and forgiveness. Thus, it is only the losers and the sinners who need salvation, repentance, and forgiveness. After all, it was not bad at all for Boston College to have a losing season so that they could realize the importance of divine revelation.

I came back to Santa Clara in December 2016 for Christmas break, but Father Schall wrote to me that he would be away for Christmas vacation with his brother. I stopped in Santa Clara on the way to Seattle for the formation gathering, so I could not wait for Father Schall to return from Christmas vacation.

Thanks be to God, I had the opportunity to go back to California in late March 2017. I submitted a paper at the 2017 Twentieth Annual Conference of Law, Culture, and Humanities hosted by Stanford Law School. The Organizing Committee accepted my paper titled "Scalia v. Aquinas: The Battle of Legal Interpretation." I emailed Father Schall and tried to set a date in advance to meet him in Los Gatos. I also explained to Father Schall about my visit to California and my paper at Stanford.

"I am usually here! Glad to hear of the paper. I never thought Scalia a Thomist," wrote Father Schall.

---

[36] James V. Schall, S.J., *Reasonable Pleasures: The Strange Coherences of Catholicism* (San Francisco: St. Ignatius Press, 2013), 71.

The problem was I only had a tiny window to meet Father Schall during the conference. I was proposing to see him for dinner on Saturday at Los Gatos, but it turned out that his grandniece was picking him up for dinner that evening. Finally, we agreed to meet for breakfast on Saturday morning before I left for Stanford's conference.

It was my first breakfast with Father Schall. We sat at a private table in the dining room of the Sacred Heart Center. "I usually have oatmeal for my breakfast, but feel free to grab any hot breakfast that you like," said Father Schall.

While enjoying our breakfast, Father Schall asked me, "Have you been to Assumption College in Worcester?"

"No."

"You should visit the Assumption College and find Marc Guerra there."

Guerra was a professor of theology and the editor of a festschrift in honor of Father Schall titled, *Jerusalem, Athens, and Rome*, published by St. Augustine Press. Father Schall seemed to want me to connect with him because I might learn something from him.

"Tell me more about the paper that you are going to present at Stanford. I didn't know that Scalia is a Thomist."

"Scalia is not a Thomist, but I am writing about his legal thought in comparison with Aquinas' Treatise on Law."

I then explained my paper; on January 7, 2016, Justice Scalia delivered his last public lecture, titled "Saint Thomas Aquinas and Law." Many have criticized Scalia for having an anachronistic reading of Aquinas. But I think that those analysts had missed seeing that Scalia was searching for a deeper meaning instead of chastising Aquinas's theory of law. I wanted to investigate whether Aquinas's theological insights and Scalia's jurisprudence showed similar traits. My argument was that although Scalia's jurisprudence is not identical to Aquinas's theology, their positions are much closer than people would immediately imagine. For instance, they shared similar views on the limits of judicial authority, and a reasonable judge must avoid sentimentality and personal values in judging.

"So you are writing on Aquinas's Treatise on Law?"

"Yes, the point of departure of my paper is comparing Aquinas's Treatise on Law and Scalia's textualism."

"Did you talk about Aquinas' idea of justice in your paper?"

"No, why do you ask that."

"People always talk about justice these days when they talk about law; for Aquinas, justice, like politics, has a proper place in the order of things, but not the highest."

"Father Schall, I would like to hear more of your thoughts about it, so please explain it to me."

Father Schall then explained that Aquinas's Treatise on Law was hugely different from what was listed as law in the legal textbooks or what we learned in law school. For instance, he did not include coercion as the essence of law, though he did not propose coercion was never necessary. Aquinas considered law an external principle of action, which can be distinguished from the internal principle of action, such as intellect, will, passion, and habits. The external principles of action are God, the devil, and law. As an external principle action, a good law requires the discipline of reason and virtue. Aquinas did deal with the virtue of justice, but justice is not as important as the virtue of prudence. Prudence, instead of justice, tells us specifically what to do in each case we are dealing with. Once we know the right thing to do through prudence, then we can be just.

"For Aquinas, friendship is more important than justice, even in political life," stated Father Schall.

"Oh, I never thought about the connection between justice and friendship."

Father Schall explained further that when Aquinas discusses the highest Christian virtue, that is charity, he did not base his discussion on justice but rather on friendship. The problem with justice is that it looks to the abstract relationship between persons, what is due or not due, not the persons themselves. But friendship and charity look primarily to the person who is an object of our friendship and love. So charity cannot be assumed entirely under the virtue of justice, because justice only directs us into abstract relationships but not to persons.

Again, whenever I had a conversation with Father Schall, I needed humility to admit how much I didn't know. The idea of justice and friendship was not the topic of my paper; nevertheless, I was grateful for the insight from Father Schall. I hoped that I could further explore the idea of prudence in my comparison of Aquinas's law and Scalia's textualism.

"Do you have a plan to publish your paper?"

"I hope so, but I still need to do a lot of work on it, and I could not find the original text of Scalia's last lecture."

"How come?"

I explained that Justice Scalia delivered his last lecture on Aquinas at the Dominican House of Studies before he died. I contacted the Dominicans about the text, but they said that it was not available. In the meantime, Scalia's family already donated all of his papers to Harvard Law School and they were not available to the public yet. What I was doing so far was relying on secondary sources about the text.

Father Schall replied, "Do you remember Cindy Searcy?"

"Yes."

"She is pretty resourceful among legal circles in DC; she might be able to help you."

"Okay, I will check with her about it."

Father Schall continued, "Speaking about publication, I want to give you my latest book."

Father Schall showed me his book titled, *Catholicism and Intelligence,* published by Emmaus Road Publishing.

"I want you to write a review of this book."

"I will do my best, Father Schall."

"Are you going to Stanford directly from here?"

"Yes, I have to present my paper at 11am."

"I went to Stanford a few months ago to meet an old friend. Another friend drove me there. We got lost when we were trying to find our meeting spot. It was like finding a needle in a haystack because the campus is so huge. So it's better for you to leave now," said Fr. Schall.

We finished our breakfast and wrapped up our meeting. Father Schall suddenly said, "I presume that you won't have time to watch the basketball game this afternoon?"

On Saturday, April 1, Gonzaga's men's basketball team would play against South Carolina in the Final Four of the NCAA Men's

Basketball tournament. Both teams were making their first-ever Final Four appearance. The game between Gonzaga and South Carolina would be at 3 PM Mountain Standard Time, which was around 2 PM Pacific Standard Time. As much as I would have loved to see the game, I would still be attending my conference at Stanford.

I replied to Father Schall, "Well, I hope that Gonzaga can win the game this afternoon so I can watch them play in the final on Tuesday."

"When we were at St. Michael, none of us could imagine that Gonzaga would play in a national championship. We will see whether they can win the championship."

We finished our conversation, and I said goodbye to Father Schall before heading to Stanford.

The Twenty-Fourth Saturday

On the Death of a Great Scholar

The Spring semester in Boston College went by quickly, and it was time for me to head back for summer break. I decided to go back to Santa Clara for summer; my main project that summer was to finish my book manuscript. My Rector, Father James Gartland, S.J., granted me permission to work on my manuscript. Thanks be to God, I finally secured a contract from Routledge publishing.

I arrived in Santa Clara on the evening of May 23, 2017. On the following day, I received the news of the death of a political scientist, Peter Lawler. I met Peter Lawler during my sojourn at Notre Dame. At that time, he gave a talk on "Lost in the Cosmos - Did Walker Percy Really Write the Last Self-Help Book?" I knew that Lawler was a good friend of Father Schall. I emailed Father Schall right away; first, I wanted to tell him that I was back in California, and I hoped to see him soon. Second, it must be a shock for Father Schall to hear about the sudden death of Peter Lawler. Father Schall just replied with a short message from his iPhone, "I am in Dallas."

I could not wait to see Father Schall, but I had to go to Los Angeles in the first week of June to attend the priestly Ordination of the Jesuit priests. I did not try to see Father Schall until the second week of June. When I checked if he was available for a visit, he wrote me back, "I am going down to La La land today and returning in a week." I am a bit surprised to hear the news because Father Schall had just been in Dallas two weeks earlier, and now he was heading to Los Angeles.

It was not until Saturday, July 1, that I finally visited Father Schall. I came to his room before lunch time, and we had time to chat for a little bit. I asked Father Schall of his doings.

"I have pneumonia," he said.

"Are you okay Father Schall?"

"I have some difficulties breathing and I can't walk for too long."

I thought maybe his health issues were caused by his busy travel schedule in the past week. It must be tiring for an 89 year old man like him to make a trip to Dallas and then Los Angeles in three weeks.

"I can come back another day if you want to rest."

"No, I am okay."

Father Schall then asked me how was my first year of theological studies in Boston College. I told him that it was not bad at all; there were some issues in the theological center, but I had a decent theological education overall. I took three classes on Aquinas in the last one year: Introduction to Aquinas, Comparison between Aquinas and Augustine, and Theological Virtues, which was pretty much about Aquinas theory on virtue. Also, I had taken several classes on the Bible. In the end, it depended on whether you could pick excellent theological courses at Boston College.

Father Schall seemed pleased to hear that I learned about Aquinas, and he recommended I take more classes on St. Augustine. "Our Society will be much stronger and better if we spent more time reading Saint Augustine than the *New York Times*," he said. Here Father Schall was referring to the Society of Jesus.

"Oh yes, Father Schall, I finally read the entire book of Augustine's *Confession* during my eight-day retreat last month."

"Glad to hear it. Maybe for your next retreat, you can read the *City of God*."

I switched the topic of our conversation with a question, "Father Schall, were you surprise to hear of the death of Peter Lawler?" I shared with Father Schall my encounter with Peter Lawler a year before in Notre Dame and how he commented on the sudden death of Justice Scalia. I remember Peter Lawler said "We don't know when we will die; look at what happened with Scalia, he just dropped dead without any warning." Lawler was referring to the death of Justice Scalia, who died a few months earlier. About a year later, it was Lawler's turn to face his Maker.

"No one can survive death; Peter Lawler knew about it," said Father Schall.

He paused for a moment and asked me, "Did you read his last book on *American Heresies and Higher Education*?"

"No."

In a somber tone, Father Schall explained that in his last book, Lawler pointed out that most of the world's utopian projects want to eliminate death. Nevertheless, the notion of bypassing death is contrary to the Christian doctrine of the resurrection of the body that our lives will be completed eternally after death.

Father Schall paused for a moment and continued, "He was a dynamo; it's a big loss for the intellectual community in this country."

Father Schall gave high praise for Peter Lawler. Although he was just a professor at a small private Christian college in North Georgia,

Berry College, somehow he managed to see the whole country and what goes on in it better than many professors in big universities. Moreover, he could also understand the souls of this nation and our own souls better than most of us.

"You must read that book if you want to get to work in the University," said Father Schall.

Father Schall then tried to explicate Lawler's argument that higher education is aristocratic. It is primarily designed to find out who is best. Most students come to college without any capacity to discover the truth, and, therefore, the capacity to be liberally educated is given to relatively few students. So the notion that everyone should obtain a doctoral degree, law degree, or MD is unrealistic and harmful to those who must study beyond their natural capacities.

Lawler saw that a "liberal" education today has little relation to the classical notion of "liberal education" where one can find a real discussion about the truth, God, human beings, the cosmos, and their relationships. Universities these days have become the least diverse institutions in society, with little freedom being allowed to challenge diversity and political correctness. The political agenda of the American universities is then exported to the political institutions, courts, and culture.

"The book is also important for you to learn to be a good teacher," said Father Schall.

Father Schall expounded his view that the students in Berry College were blessed to have Lawler as their teacher. Lawler believed that a good teacher must focus on the texts, so there should be only a professor, students, and a good book or text in the classroom. Powerpoints, laptops, smartphones must be prohibited in the classroom.

At the end of the day, what we need is a Platonic model of education where the master and the student discuss in a serious way a deep concern for each other's souls and the question of what the truth is.

We finished our conversation and then moved to the dining room for lunch. We sat at a public table with other Jesuits, and one of them was Father Schall's good friend, Father Ken Baker. I met Fr. Baker many years ago at the Jesuit villa on Hayden Lake during our summer break. At that time, he was still living in New Jersey and working as the Editor of Homiletic and Pastoral Review. But he retired to Los Gatos. We were discussing many issues, including the appointment of a Spanish Jesuit, the then Archbishop Luis Ladaria, S.J., as the new Prefect of CDF.

"Ken, do you know anything about this Ladaria man?" asked Father Schall to Father Baker.

"I don't know much about him; someone who should about know about him is Navone. But he is not around anymore."

Father Baker was referring to the late Father John Navone, S.J., another good friend of Father Schall, who died in December 2016. Father Navone was a great theologian who spent many years teaching at Gregorian University in Rome. Father Navone was not only a gifted theologian, but he also knew the details of the Church's politics in Rome.

"Probably Navone would say that now the Church is controlled by Spaniards," said Father Schall.

"Yes, that Navone would probably say; typical Navone with his corky genius." Father Baker continued, "Navone was not only genius, but he could also be sneaky too. I remember when we arrived in Rome, Navone suddenly disappeared from the immigration line.

It turned out that he had an Italian passport; he went to a special line for Italian citizens and left us behind."

"I wish that he could have come here to spend time with us."

"Do you know his last wishes when he was lying in the hospital before his death?"

"What did he ask?"

"He asked to drink a particular beer that he liked and to have his favorite ice cream, and then he died on the following day."

We all laughed to hear the story and continued our lunch. After lunch, I told Father Schall that I would be in Santa Clara until the end of July, and I was hoping to see him again next week. Father Schall then walked with me until we reached the Sacred Heart Center's main door and said, "I will stop here; sorry that I can't walk with you to your car." Of course, I understood his health situation, and I said goodbye to Father Schall.

The Twenty-Fifth Saturday

On Tocqueville in Arabia

After my last meeting with Father Schall, I began to contemplate that his health had seemed to decline, and he would turn 90 next year. I might not have much time to spend with this great man. I only had a few more weeks in California because I had to go to Denver at the end of July for the so-called Arrupe experience. The Arrupe experience was a three-week retreat designed for the Jesuits who were about to be ordained as deacons or priests; it was a kind of final preparation for Ordination. I hoped that I would have a few more visits with Father Schall.

On the following Saturday, I did not waste my time and drove to Los Gatos to pay a visit to Father Schall. As usual, he welcomed me into his room. I asked him how his health was. He said that his health was improving but the doctor advised him not to travel long-distance any longer.

When I came to the room earlier, I saw that Father Schall was reading a book. I asked him what book he was reading. He showed me the book, titled *Tocqueville in Arabia*. Father Schall explained that the author of the book, Joshua Mitchell, was his colleague at Georgetown Governmental Studies. The year Father Schall left Georgetown, Mitchell published the book. Somehow, Father Schall had missed reading it, but recently his friends, a couple that he had known for many years, sent him a copy.

The book itself is a reflection on Tocqueville's famous book, *Democracy in America*. But the author tries to explain why Tocqueville has not been known in the Arab world. In some way, the book attempts to cover many different aspects: education, philosophy, history, theology, political theory, commentary on Plato, Aristotle, and was also an autobiography.

"Have you read Tocqueville's *Democracy in America*?" asked Father Schall.

"I had read fragments of the book in graduate school, but I never read the work in its entirety."

For the second time, I embarrassed myself by admitting that I gained a doctorate in Comparative Constitutional Law without ever having read *Democracy in America*. During my sojourn at Notre Dame, I met a nice young lady who was a first-year law student at Notre Dame. She already read the entire text of *Democracy in America* during her undergraduate years at the University of Dallas. One day, we ended up having a conversation about Tocqueville, and I had to admit my handicap of not having read Tocqueville's magisterial work.

"Nobody cares about Tocqueville these days," said Father Schall.

He continued, "Mitchell's book can be helpful to attract students to reading classical literature."

"I will put the book in my reading list," I told Father Schall.

"Having read the book itself is not enough; the more important thing is that you must have the desire to know and learn," remind Father Schall.

He continued, "Maybe someday you can write something about Tocqueville in Indonesia."

"Why do you make such a suggestion?"

"Well, Indonesia is the largest Muslim country, so it may be fitting to analyze democracy in Indonesia like Mitchel did in the Middle East."

"Maybe someday I can write something like that, but I must read the books first, the original Tocqueville and *Tocqueville in Arabia* that you just suggested."

"How are Muslims in Indonesia? I heard some people say Indonesian Muslims are quite different because they are moderate. I am not sure about that."

It is quite a complicated question for me, but I did my best to answer Father Schall's question. The schools of thought within Islam in Indonesian can be divided between "traditionalism" and "modernism." Traditionalism was represented by *Nahdlatul Ulama*, which tended to follow the interpretations of local religious leaders and religious teachers at Islamic boarding schools. The "modernism" was represented by Muhammadiyah, which oppose syncretism and authority of the ulama.

Nahdlatul Ulama has been praised as the advocate of moderation, compassion, anti-radicalism, inclusiveness, and tolerance. But I think the perception was built due to the achievement of the former leader of the *Nahdlatul Ulama*, the late Abdurrahman Wahid, known as Gus Dur. He was the third president of Indonesia, who was a tolerant and inclusive leader.

In recent years, however, there has been a new rising Islamic political party known as the Prosperous Justice Party (PKS), which originated from the Muslim Brotherhood movement in Indonesia.

Moreover, there had been a growth of conservative and militant Islamic organizations such as the Islamic Defenders' Front (*Front Pembela Islam*, FPI) and *Hizbut Tahir* Indonesia (HTI). These groups are firmly in favor of religious authority, expressed in the right of religious scholars (of their choosing) to interpret religious teaching and laws, and to ensure their implementation in society and politics. While these groups are relatively small, they have become the key ideologues of conservative religious ideology.

While both foreign and Indonesian scholars have tried to portray Islam in Indonesia as moderate, Islam in Indonesia is not immune from the history of violence associated with terrorism. The history of violence dates from the separatist movement of Darul Islam in the 1950s to the Borobudur Temple bombing in 1985. It was followed by the series of terror attacks in the early 2000s, which can be attributed to the Al-Qaeda-affiliated Jemaah Islamiyah Islamist terror group.

"Do you know who Charles Malik is?" asked Father Schall.

"Yes, he was a Lebanese philosopher and diplomat."

"I am impressed you know who he was."

"He was involved in drafting the UDHR, and I used some of his speeches in my class in Santa Clara a few years ago."

"Was that a class on Religion and Politics?"

"No, it was my class on Human Rights actually, so something good also came out my Human Rights class."

Father Schall just smiled and continued, "Malik said that the main intellectual link between Islam and the West was precisely Aristotle. When Aristotle has become the missing link, you know why terror can be claimed to be good."

We finished the conversation on that note and moved to the dining room for lunch. We blended in with some other Jesuits during lunch. After lunch, I said goodbye to Father Schall and told him that I was hoping to see him again the following week. "I will be here all the time this summer," said Father Schall.

The Twenty-Sixth Saturday

On G.K. Chesterton and Liturgy

I did not come back on the following Saturday because I went to San Francisco to visit a museum and walk around the city with a fellow Jesuit. But I regretted the trip as I knew I had wasted the opportunity to see Father Schall. I only had one more Saturday before heading to Denver. I emailed Father Schall and made sure that I could see him before my departure.

On July 22, 2017, I went to see Father Schall at Sacred Heart Jesuit Center. I came close to lunchtime, but I was hoping to find a private table where we could converse. I knocked on Father Schall's room, but there was no answer. After knocking on the door several times without any answer, I went down to the nursing station and checked with the nurse about Father Schall's whereabout. The nurse recommended that I go to the dining room immediately because Father Schall might already be there. I went to the dining room and saw that Father Schall was standing in the hallway in front of the dining room.

"Father Schall, I came to your room, but you were not there."

"It's close to lunchtime already, and so I was just waiting for you here."

"Sorry for not coming earlier."

"Before we eat, I want to give you my latest book on Chesterton." The book was titled *The Satisfied Crocodile: Essays on G.K. Chesterton*, published by the American Chesterton Society.

"Well, Father Schall, I haven't been able to write a review of the last book that you gave me. I am sorry for failing you."

"Don't worry. I will forgive you as long as you read the book."

We moved to the dining room and sat at a private table. As we enjoyed our lunch, Father Schall immediately asked me a question, "Have you read a lot of Chesterton?"

"I read Chesterton's *Orthodoxy* during my philosophy studies, but other than that, I haven't read a lot of his works."

"Why were you not interested in reading Chesterton?"

"Well, maybe because the writing of C.S. Lewis more influences me. Or maybe I found it hard to read *Orthodoxy* in philosophy, and it stopped me from exploring his works."

"C'mon, if you are a man of C.S. Lewis, you know what he said that if you only read a great book once, you have not read it at all."

To cover my embarrassment, I replied, "Yeah, I must reread *Orthodoxy*. But I have come across Chesterton a lot in my class on liturgy at Boston College."

"How come?"

"One of the textbooks that we used in liturgy class is the work of a Notre Dame Professor, David W. Fagerberg. He cited Chesterton a lot in his works."

"Interesting, do you remember any quotes that he uses?"

"I remember a few quotes like Chesterton said our legs have pagan origin. He said this in response to some critics who complained that Catholic liturgy has many pagan elements. Chesterton argues that humanity was human before it was Christian. Similarly, fasting and vigils were practiced by many people before Christians practiced them."

"Any Chesterton quotes that left a good impression on you?"

"There is an interesting quote that Fagerberg used in his article that was published in New Blackfriars Journal."[37]

"What is the quote?"

"I don't remember exactly; basically, Chesterton defended medieval theology and his readers loved it because they never heard of it."

"Is he using Chesterton to defend Medieval liturgy?"

"Not really, but he asked whether liturgical students could love medieval liturgy when they had never heard of it before."

"So what's his argument?"

I tried to explain the Fagerberg argument based on my memory; basically, he argues that being aware of the liturgy is not enough. More importantly, we must participate in Christ's liturgy. Although ignorance is part of the problem for the failure of human liturgical vocation, the bigger problem, according to Fagerberg, is our illicit desire, in which we desire something other than God. Liturgy is related to the story of creation. God gave human beings dominion over creation, but it is a liturgical command based on liturgical hierarchy, in which human beings would rule in accordance with God's will. But then human beings chose to follow their own will in the Garden of Eden, and by turning away from God, Adam and Eve made creation non-liturgical. Through the Incarnation, the Word became flesh to restore human beings' liturgical vocation that they

---

[37] David W. Fagerberg, "Cosmological Liturgy and a Sensible Priesthood," *New Blackfriars*, Volume 82, Issue 960, p. 76-81 (February 2001).

failed to accomplish during the Fall. The bottom line is that Fager-berg argues that to have essential knowledge and perform a proper liturgy, we must know why God created us in the first place.

"It seems that you have had a pretty decent liturgical education in Boston," said Father Schall.

"I have only learned the theory so far."

"So you haven't practiced the Mass yet?"

"Not yet, but I will do it in the Fall semester. By the way Father Schall, do you have any tips on how to learn to celebrate the Mass properly?"

Father Schall then told me that I must remember liturgy is not up to the priest to grab so that he can refashion it according to his preference. The Mass is not entertainment, but there is a tendency for many priests to want to be performers who attract laughter or applause from the congregation. A priest should not make up his own words or gestures during the Mass. The bottom line is that when a priest celebrates Mass, he should follow the rubrics and vestments indicated by the Church. Father Schall said that he heard many young priests did not wear vestments during a private Mass. He reminded me that at Mass, a priest should wear an alb, a stole, and a chasuble, and he may not con-celebrate in a secular outfit or by wearing the stole over his ordinary clerical shirt.

"Why do you think that priests nowadays tend to treat the Mass as their own personal show?" I asked Father Schall.

"The Novus Ordo Mass focused on the priest, who are now called the presider or celebrant. In the Novus Ordo, there is no emphasis on silence. People shake hands, hug, smile, and whisper. The priest can add various greetings and comments. Some priests even change the wording of important parts of the Mass."

"Do you think that Novus Ordo is kind of dubious?"

"No, that not what I meant. The last three popes have reaffirmed the validity of the Novus Ordo Mass, so there is nothing wrong with the Mass as long as you can do it properly according to what the Church has asked priests to do."

"Father Schall, I have known you for a while, but I never got a chance to join you at your private Mass."

"I usually celebrate my private Mass in the morning; you usually come late morning or afternoon. Maybe next time, you can come early in the morning. Or after your Ordination, you can come and con-celebrate with me, or I can con-celebrate at your Mass."

"What do you think about con-celebration, Father Schall? Do you think that every Jesuit priest has a right to con-celebrate Mass in the community?"

I remember that during my sojourn at Notre Dame, I was the only non-priest in the Jesuit community. All the priests usually con-celebrated the Mass during the daily liturgy; perhaps it was the only Jesuit community in the United States where every individual member of the community con-celebrated the Mass.

Father Schall replied that con-celebration is better than merely attending Mass. A priest must celebrate Mass rather than only receiving communion like the congregation. Attending a Mass cannot substitute celebrating a Mass and therefore, every priest must celebrate daily Eucharist individually.

Father Schall then said, " When you are ordained, remember that it is important that you must celebrate the Eucharist every day, even if no one is around. It's important for your spiritual life and the Church."

We spent the rest of the lunchtime discussing random stuff. After we finished lunch, I said goodbye to Father Schall. I told him that I was going to Denver on the following day for my Arrupe experience and asked his prayers for my retreat. I didn't know when I would be able to see Father Schall again. I hoped that there would be a day when I could con-celebrate a Mass with this great priest.

The Twenty-Seventh Saturday

On Poverty and the University Monastery

The Fall semester in my second year of theology flew by quickly. We were already in December and ready for Christmas break. I went back to Santa Clara and stayed there for Christmas. We did not have a long Christmas break, as all of us had to go back to Boston for our retreat right after New Year's Day. Nevertheless, I had a chance to visit Father Schall once during my short break. On that Saturday morning, I drove to Los Gatos and visited Father Schall at the Sacred Heart Center.

When we finally met, I asked Father Schall about his health. He said he was fine, but a few weeks before, he had difficulty breathing and there was some liquid in his lung. But the doctor had taken care of it, and he could breathe normally again. Then he asked me how the second year of my studies was. I said that things were getting better; in my first year, I struggled to adapt to a new life as a student again, and life in the Jesuit community and Boston were quite challenging. But the second year seemed better. Apart from enjoying my study, I enjoyed my time in Boston at a ministry for pregnant homeless women who needed shelter and support. The group was called Friends of the Unborn, which was located in Quincy, Massachusetts. In my experience, this was one of the best ministries that I'd ever had in my Jesuit formation. Often, I found myself being parachuted into a particular ministry, and the people in the ministry did not want me there. Or I found particular limitations in that I was not a priest yet. But here with Friends of the Unborn, they were welcoming and let me run my program. What I did was introduce the Spiritual Exercises of St. Ignatius of Loyola to these women. I used the daily meditation program based on the Spiritual Exercises, written by the late Jesuit Father, Mark Link, S.J. I had no illusion that these women would be able to learn the Spiritual Exercises, but at least, I could invite them to be more reflective and start to have some spiritual conversation. Overall, the Maternity Home offered many programs that aimed to help women walk on their own feet after giving birth. My program was just a complimentary program for those young ladies.

"It looks like a good program; maybe they should add a program for those ladies to learn from the rich," said Father Schall.

Father Schall then made an analogy that the vows of poverty and chastity originating from the monastic tradition did not mean that richness and sex in married life are bad, but both are good. Father Schall explained that marriage is basically about friendship and it closely relates to *eros*. He pointed out that how Plato and Aristotle bring up the relation of *eros* to *philia*, as well as of both to some end or purpose. The bottom line is that sexual intimacy is one of the keys to having a healthy, functional and happy relationship in married life.

Concerning wealth, Father Schall explained that being wealthy was good because it is about how to think properly. If we do not think properly, we won't be able to achieve the goals of abundance. In Father Schall's view, with the right mindset, we will be able to invent, invest, experiment, change, and take risks, and, moreover, we will know how to save money and becoming debt free. In other words, being wealthy requires a knowledge of how wealth is produced and innovatively distributed. In the end, being wealthy in healthy way is part of what the Incarnation taught us, that Christ was taking a risk in being human like us but at the same time He respects our freedom.

The achievement of abundant wealth is the product of taking the risks and at the same time respecting the promise of freedom in our human relationships with one another.

I switched the topic of our conversation, "Speaking about the Monastic tradition, I want to ask you something, Father Schall. You were supposed to give a keynote address at St. Gregory University earlier this year. I heard that you did not make it because of your health. But now the University closed. What do you think about it?"

St. Gregory's University was located in Shawnee, Oklahoma, and the Benedictine monks founded it in 1875. The University closed its operations at the end of Fall 2017.

"Yeah, I did not make it there. The doctor advised me not to travel at that time. I heard that they did not have enough money to run the operation and must close their business. Have you ever been to St. Gregory?"

"Yes, I visited the place last summer, after my Arrupe experience."

"Were you giving a paper?"

"No, actually, it was because my friend John Rosselle; you might remember him? He came to visit you a few years ago. He left the Jesuits and got married. I visited him last summer, and his wife is an alumna of St. Gregory University. Then we visited St. Gregory during my short visit in Oklahoma."

"Sorry to hear about John; did he leave because of this St. Gregory woman?"

"No, he met her after he left the Jesuits. He left for many reasons, but one of them was that he just wanted to have a woman in his life. But he does not know the hard reality of married life. I think he is just like a little boy who wants to have a puppy, but he doesn't know what to do with it. I warned him, but he did not listen to my words."

"There is nothing you could do if he already made up his mind."

"I am curious about St. Gregory because I thought Monastic tradition usually has the tradition of in-house education instead of building a university."

"I wrote about it in my book *The Praise of Sons of Bitches*."

"I heard about the book, but it was already out of print."

"Fingerhut and St. Augustine Press are planning to re-publish it."

Father Schall then explained that the monastery, the University, and the city are related in prayer and politics. The Benedictines believe that the worship of God and the brotherhood are the prerequisites to obtaining knowledge. The monastery itself was a sign of rejection of the heresy, which identifies divine purpose with worldly affairs. But the monks were not fleeing the world, but instead, they were engaging with the world from a monastery. The monastery is the transcendent center, which transcends the world. A monastery is a place to worship God, pursue truth, and a place of brotherly love; the University and the city must also embody what the monastery stands for. The bottom line is that a university must not become a monastery, but it should be a place where its members can worship God, pursue truth, and share brotherly love.

There was nothing special and exciting during the rest of our conversation that afternoon. After lunch, I told Father Schall I wanted to ask him little favor regarding another book project of mine. In the last year, I had also been working on a festschrift in honor of the late Father Robert Araujo, S.J., who died in 2015. Thanks be to God, I had also secured a contract for the festschrift; it was to be published by the Franciscan University Press of Steubenville, titled *Priests, Lawyers, and Scholars.* A few months before, I asked Father Schall to write a foreword for the book, and now I needed Father Schall to sign a contract for the publication of his essay. Father Schall just grabbed the pen from the front desk of the Sacred Heart Center and signed the contract.

Father Schall then decided to walk with me to my car. I asked him if he was okay to step outside. He said that he was fine and wanted to walk outside a little bit. As we walked together, I told him that I was still waiting for approval for my priestly Ordination, and I asked his prayers. Father Schall assured me that he would pray for me. As I drove away, looking in the rear-view mirror, I could see Father Schall walking slowly toward the Grotto.

On His 90th Birthday

On January 20, 2018, Father Schall turned 90 years old. I wrote an essay that became an inspiration for this book, entitled *"Saturdays with Father Schall: A Young Jesuit on the Older Jesuit's 90th Birthday,"* published by the *Catholic World Report*.

On January 23, 2018, Father Schall wrote me an email that I will cite in its entirety:

Someone sent me the CWR comment on JVS that you kindly did. I appreciated your listening to Schall rambles and your setting this down. You have been a good friend and I have appreciated your attention and coming by and keeping in touch. In point of fact, I have never really had anything to do with the education of Jesuits old or young, except in the sense that one or the other might have read something I wrote someplace.

You caught the spirit of what I have to say in your remarks on the Sertillanges book. The relative abandonment of the intellectual life and its replacement with social activism is the heart of the issue. If you neglect the first, the second will never be right.

Keep in touch, and again, thanks for your kind words, pray for me, Jim.

There are a few interesting facts from Father Schall's email. First, again, he showed his humility by not taking credit for being a good model to many young Jesuits. Indeed, he was never really involved in any formal capacity in the education of any young Jesuits, but his life and works have influenced at least a small number of young Jesuits.

Second, I was a bit pleasantly surprised that Father Schall had been considering me his good friend. I regarded Father Schall as a good mentor and a father figure, but I never really thought to consider him a friend. Nevertheless, at one point, I wondered whether he considered me a friend, and the answer was yes. I will be forever grateful for Father Schall, who was willing to be a friend to me.

In a follow-up conversation, I expressed my gratitude to Father Schall for his generosity in being friends with an Indonesian-born Jesuit like myself. He then wrote me back, saying that he was grateful to have two Indonesian friends in his life: John Riyadi and me. Again, John Riyadi is the crown prince of the Lippo business empire, one of the largest conglomerates in Indonesia. And as for me, I am just a son of a poor miner from an obscure island in Indonesia. While Riyadi is the CEO in-waiting, as he will assume the throne of his family business empire, I was just waiting to be ordained as a priest. Nevertheless, there is an interesting similarity between Riyadi and myself in that we are both "post-Indonesian generations" and friends of Father Schall.

Not long after Father Schall's birthday, I received the good news that my petition for the Sacrament of Holy Orders had been approved. I would be ordained a deacon in September 2018, followed by priestly ordination in June 2019. At the same time, there had been a discussion with the Provincial Superior about what I would do after ordination. The Provincial was considering that I do a pastoral year instead of applying for a job at the University. The Provincial was asking me to consider the possibility of going to Alaska and serving there as a priest.

I wrote to Father Schall and informed him that I had obtained approval for the Sacrament of Holy Orders. I also shared that Provincial did not want me to work at the University or teach right away. He wanted me to do a pastoral year and was considering sending me to Alaska for my pastoral year.

Father Schall wrote back to me,

I am not surprised about the 'pastoral year' -- no clue at this end of the importance of knowledge. A year in Alaska would probably not be all bad, but not ideal.

I was a bit surprised to hear Father Schall's statement; I thought he would be critical to the Provincial's idea to send me to Alaska. He often reminded me that I should not wait too long to start my academic endeavors because I was not that young. Honestly, I was not incredibly happy with the Provincial's idea, and I was hoping that Father Schall would come to my defense. But his statement was a bit ambiguous.

I did not understand why Father Schall seemed indifferent toward the pastoral year. I guess that he wanted to remind me that we do not always get what we want, and that there are still unexpected blessings from our unwanted experiences. More importantly, Father Schall might have wanted to remind me about the Vow of Obedience that I pronounced in the Society of Jesus.

I never asked Father Schall why he thought the Alaska experience would not be bad for me. Father Schall considered me his friend and had been a good friend to me in the past few years. When a good priest-scholar like Father Schall concluded that a year in

Alaska was not a bad experience, I should pay attention to his message. A good friend does not always say something that you want to hear, and I think Father Schall played the role of a good friend by reminding me I should be obedient to God's will as expressed through my Provincial Superior.

The Twenty-Eighth Saturday

On Gilson and the Great Cathedrals

In May 2018, I finished my spring semester of the second year of theological studies, and again, I came back to Santa Clara University Jesuit Community for the summer. Though I didn't have a good experience during my regency assignment in Santa Clara, in some way, I considered that place as my "home," and I came back regularly to that place. My plan for the summer was to finish my article on Justice Scalia's last lecture on Aquinas and maybe work on another writing project.

I had to make my eight-day silent retreat in Mundelein Seminary and then attended a priestly ordination of a fellow Jesuit, Henry Shea, at Fordham University. It was already early June when I arrived in Santa Clara. I emailed Father Schall that I was back in Santa Clara and planning to see him. He wrote me back that his brother was dying and he might have to travel to Idaho for the funeral, so he asked me to re-confirm on Friday before my visit. On the day before my visit, I confirmed with Father Schall about my visit, and he said that he would be at Los Gatos and that I could come for lunch.

I arrived at the Sacred Heart Jesuit Center before lunchtime and went to Father Schall's room on the second floor. I knocked on the door but there was no answer, I knocked harder several times and still no response. I went to the dining room to see if Father Schall was already there, but he wasn't around. I checked with the nurse on call in the nursing station to see if Father Schall left that morning, but she said that Father Schall was there. So, I went back to the room and knocked on the door again; finally, I decided to open the door slowly and saw the computer was on. I went into the room, and Father Schall came out from the restroom at around the same time. Both of us were surprised to see each other.

"Sorry for entering your room Father Schall. I knocked your door many times, but there was no answer."

"The batteries of my hearing aid are dead, so I could not hear." Father Schall then asked my help to replace the batteries of his hearing aid, and I found it a humbling experience to help this great priest. I never noticed before that Father Schall had been wearing a hearing aid. I guess we should treasure the gift of hearing as one of the most beautiful miracles in our lives and accept with grace when God has taken away that gift.

After I finished replacing the batteries, Father Schall put the hearing aid back and then we moved to the dining room for lunch. We could not find a private table, so we sat with other Jesuits at a big table. One of the Jesuits who sat at the same table with us was Father James Felt, S.J., who taught at Santa Clara University for 41 years.

"Do you know Father Felt?" asked Father Schall of me.

"I heard many stories about you at the Santa Clara Jesuit community," I said to Father Felt.

"I hope that you heard many good stories about me. You worked at Santa Clara?"

"I did my regency there a few years ago; I came to Santa Clara right after you left for Los Gatos in Spring 2013. I inherited many of the philosophy books that you left behind."

"Did you take over my old room?"

"No, your books were displayed at the Nobili Hall, and so I took many of them, especially your collection on Gilson."

"You must read Gilson very well, then?" Father Schall interjected.

"I haven't read all of them," I replied with embarrassment.

"This year is the 100th anniversary of Gilson's lectures on Aquinas," said Father Schall.[38]

He then asked me, "Have you ever read his famous lectures on Aquinas' philosophy?"

"Not entirely, only small fragment of it. I took a class on Aquinas on God, and apart from reading the *Summa*, I also read a few parts of Gilson's lectures."

"Your theological education is not bad at all. What other classes on Aquinas did you take that year?"

"I took another class on Aquinas' theology on Grace."

"Keep taking classes on Aquinas while you have the opportunity."

"I have two semesters left, and I will see if I can take a few more classes on Aquinas."

An elderly man who sat at the same table with us interspersed in his low voice, "It looks that the Society has a bright future with a man like you." Honestly, I do not know if an outlier like me can represent the future of the Society of Jesus. I do not have any ambition

---

[38] Father Schall was referring to the series of Gilson lectures which later appeared as *Le Thomisme: introduction au système de Saint Thomas d 'Aquin.*

to be the leader, and I do not think I will be appointed as the leader of the Jesuits in the future.

"I don't think that I can be compared to your generation. You had a superb philosophy education in Mount St. Michael and I just had a mediocre philosophy education in Chicago," I said to those Jesuits.

I continued with my rant, "I read somewhere that when Gilson came to visit Mount St. Michael, he was impressed by the philosophy collection, especially the medieval literature."

Father Schall replied, "Oh yeah, he even stated that he would prefer St. Michael over any school in the world."

"Where is that collection now?"

"They moved it to Gonzaga first before they closed down the program. You could ask Bernie here, as the former President of Gonzaga, where are those collections?"

Father Bernie Coughlin, S.J., was the former president of Gonzaga University, and he sat at the same table with us. Father Coughlin then replied, "I think that most of them are in the rare book collections at the Foley library."

"If you have such a special collection, you should make Gonzaga a center of medieval philosophy study in the world."

"We didn't have the money to run that kind of a program. We needed to use our limited resources for different purposes."

"Like building a basketball program," said Father Schall.

"Gonzaga is not only basketball," Father Coughlin replied.

We finished the conversation on that note and resumed our lunch. After lunch, some Jesuits left our table while we stayed for dessert and further conversation. I resume the conversation with Father Schall by saying:

"I wish that we Jesuits could benefit from those special collections."

"I heard that the collections were neglected for many years, and it was not until Spitzer came that he began to fund electronic cataloging of the books," said Father Schall.

Father Schall was referring to Father Robert Spitzer, S.J., the former President of Gonzaga University. In 2003, Father Spitzer funded the Library Committee to report in detail on the collection and on steps to be taken toward its electronic cataloging. In 2006, Father Spitzer began the project with the goal to achieving the electronic cataloging of the collections.[39]

"Well, although we may really not appreciate those collections any longer, perhaps people from outside Catholic circles will appreciate it and use it for their research," I said.

Father Schall replied, "you know that when they build St. Mary Cathedral in San Francisco, many Catholics complained that the new Cathedral cost so much money. But it was the Jews and Protestants who said to me that the Cathedral was the most glorious thing in the city."

Father Schall paused for a moment and continued, "Have you visited St. Mary's Cathedral in San Francisco?"

"I visited St. Mary's Cathedral many years ago when I was a novice. We did a tour in Northern California and we visited St. Mary's

---

[39] See Rare Book Collections: Introduction to The Gonzaga Collection, https://researchguides.gonzaga.edu/c.php?g=67719&p=1548937

Cathedral. Some of my fellow Jesuit novices did not like it because they said it's too modern, but I like it."

"St. Mary's Cathedral is one of the most beautiful cathedrals in our time. I wrote about the history of its construction and its architecture."

"Where did you write about it."

"It was a chapter in the *Praise of Sons of Bitches*."

"When the new edition of the book will be available?"

"I don't know, Fingerhut said that he would re-print the book soon, but it seems to take him forever to publish it."

We finished dessert and moved out of the dining room. I said goodbye to Father Schall. He walked with me to my car; I told Father Schall that I hoped to come back again next Saturday if he was around. He said that he would be around, but it would depend on his brother's condition, and again, he asked me to check first before coming to visit.

The Twenty-Ninth Saturday

On the Death of a Sibling

I checked with Father Schall on the following Friday on whether he was available for a visit on Saturday. He replied that he would be around, and I could come to visit. I drove to Los Gatos on Saturday morning, and as usual, I went to Father Schall's room upon my arrival. I knocked on the door, and I heard Father Schall's voice, "Come in." I opened the door and saw Father Schall sitting at his desk. He said, "My brother just died this morning; sorry that I did not have a chance to tell you. I have many things to take care of now, so you can go lunch by yourself and join those ancient fathers."

I told Father Schall that I was sorry for his loss, and I would give him some space. I went to the dining room and had lunch with the other Jesuits. It felt weird to have lunch without Father Schall. I did not stay for too long and went back to Santa Clara immediately after lunch.

I wanted to give Father Schall some space, so I did not come back to visit Los Gatos until the 4th of July weekend. More than two weeks had passed since his brother's death, so I presume that Father Schall was already back home. The Jesuits at the Sacred Heart Center had a barbeque on that day, so I went there for the BBQ dinner, hoping to see Father Schall.

After arriving in Los Gatos, I went to Father Schall's room and knocked on his door, but no answer. I thought the battery of his hearing aid might have died again and so I slowly opened the door, but he was not there and his computer was off. I went to the nursing station and checked on Father Schall's whereabouts; the nurse said that Father Schall was probably already in the backyard for the social hour before the BBQ. I went there and saw that Father Schall was already sitting with some other Jesuits. I said hi to him, but I could not join him at the same table because the table was already full. I told Father Schall I would try to find him after dinner.

I sat with some other Jesuits during dinner, and after we finished with our meal, I saw that Father Schall had already gone back to his room. I went to Father Schall's room and tried to have a little conversation. I was hoping at least to check on how Father Schall was doing.

I asked Father Schall how his brother's funeral was. He answered that I must read his piece in the *Catholic World Report*, in which he published his sermon from his brother's funeral.

"He was a good man and lived a good life," said Father Schall about his brother.

"He was your younger brother, right?"

"Yes, he was six years younger than me, and he could never have predicted his eldest brother would outlive him."

"So, two of you were very close?"

"We were pretty close, and I considered him one of my closest friends."

"I never thought that we could consider our sibling as a friend."

"You did not consider your sister as your friend?"

"Honestly, no. I think the relationship between siblings is different than friendship. I do not know; maybe because I have a kind of love and hate relationship with my sister."

"So, you were not that close to your sister?"

"We were kind of close, although there are a lot of problems in our relationship. But my point is that with our siblings, we are kind of stuck and have no choice, while with our friends, we can always pick and choose or refuse to be friends with others."

We finished our conversation on that note. I didn't want to stay for too long because it was already around 8 PM, and I wanted to give Father Schall time to rest. I went back to Santa Clara, hoping to see Father Schall again soon.

On the Thirtieth Saturday

We Never Say Goodbye

I did not come back on the following Saturday because I spent the weekend of July 14 -15 in the Jesuit villa in the Santa Cruz mountains with a fellow Jesuit. Part of the reason for us going to the villa was to watch the final World Cup between France and Croatia. Again, I was regretting my decision to not spend my Saturday visiting Father Schall. I could have watched the game in Santa Clara instead of going to Santa Cruz.

After returning to Santa Clara, I emailed Father Schall and told him that I was planning to visit him on the following Saturday afternoon, July 21. He wrote me back, "I will be around, but I want to watch the British Open." I thought that since Father Schall wanted to watch the British Open, it would be better to come later in the evening for supper. I went to the Sacred Heart Center before supper and knocked at Father Schall's room. "Come in," he said. I opened the door and saw Father Schall was sitting on his computer and writing.

"I thought you would come for lunch," said Father Schall.

"Well, you said that you wanted to watch the British Open, so I decided to come in the evening."

"Sorry for the confusion."

"I am also sorry because I did not clarify it with you first. Is that okay for me to visit now?"

"That's fine, please take a seat."

I sat on a chair in Father Schall's room and asked how his health was. He said that he was doing well. Maybe it was just unfounded and un-intelligible observation, but Father Schall's skin looked pale. I hoped that he was doing fine, but I didn't want to express my observation.

"Did you watch the British Open? asked Father Schall.

"No. I don't know how to play golf, and so I don't know the rules. I just watch the World Cup."

"You may be taking the better part. The World Cup finals would probably be watched by half of the population of the world. Maybe only around 5 million people or less watched the British Open."

Father Schall then switched the conversation by asking me how my writing was going. I told him that I almost finished my long article on St. Thomas Aquinas and Justice Scalia, and hopefully, I would be able to publish it in the coming year. I just needed to find a law review that would be interested in publishing it. Then he asked, "What's next for you after this summer?"

"I will be ordained as a deacon in September, so I am getting ready for the Diaconate and then priestly ordination."

"Have you ever read Cardinal Muller's book on *Priesthood and Diaconate*?"

"No."

"You must read the book before your ordination. Muller has many good insights into the Sacrament of Holy Orders."

" I read Joseph Ratzinger's collection of homilies on priestly and diaconate ordination."

"Good, you can read both. Muller is Ratzinger, and Ratzinger is Muller."

"Father Schall, do you have any personal tips on the final preparation for the ordinations, both as a deacon and a priest?"

"Keep learning; you must have an ongoing relationship with scholarly theology even after your ordination."

"Do you think the crisis that we face today is because we do not have many learned priests?"

"I tend to think both Church and State are in terrible situations, probably worse for the Church because many priests do not know what to believe in anymore." Father Schall paused for a moment and continued, "Look at the debate over divorces, remarriage, and communion. They want to move something in the realm of spiritual direction to the confession."

Father Schall explained that in the spiritual direction, a priest can give practical advice and guidance for divorced or remarried people to adjust their spiritual life of marriage in order to keep it effective and on track. This is a solid advice, but it is noticeably different than a confession, in which Christ provides sacramental grace to our soul through the ministry of His priest. So, in the confession, a priest cannot dilute the sacramental grace by providing some practical advice on how to live a good life as a remarried or divorced person.

I understood Father Schall's message; indeed, I would be ordained when many of the faithful have become more and more confused about what the Church teaches. In my first two years of theological studies, I began to see more and more people ignoring the doctrines, while following the doctrines of the Church was now considered unloving.

We finished our conversation on that note, and then Father Schall invited me to go to the dining room for supper. Before we moved for supper, Father Schall gave me his latest book titled *On Islam: A Chronological Record, 2002-2018*, published by Ignatius Press. We moved to the dining room and joined the other Jesuits for supper. We did not have any interesting topics to discuss for the rest of the evening. Father Schall walked with me to my car after supper, and I drove back to Santa Clara. Little did I know, it turned out that evening was my last Saturday with Father Schall, and I did not even have a chance to say goodbye formally.

On the Time to Say Goodbye

After my last meeting with Father Schall, I did not have a chance to visit him again. On the following week, I went camping with some friends at Sequoia National Park. On the weekend after, there was a farewell BBQ party for an Indonesian Jesuit who just finished his theological studies at the Graduate Theological Union in Berkeley. On the weekend after that, there was a Jesuit West Province gathering at Santa Clara University. It was a kind of mandatory meeting so I could not skip the conference. I left for Boston immediately after the Province gathering because I had to help in the Church where I was about to start my diaconate service. I felt terrible that I did not have a chance to say goodbye to Father Schall. I emailed Father Schall and said I was sorry that I did not have an opportunity to visit him before returning to Boston. Father Schall replied and said that there was no need to say sorry, and he wished me all the best for my final year of theological studies.

In the first week of my fall semester, Ryan Anderson, a Senior Research Fellow at The Heritage Foundation, posted a negative tweet about Father Schall's book *On Islam*. Anderson tweeted as follows:

"Fr. Schall's collection of essays on Islam and violence suffers from reductionist arguments, nonexistent evidence, and historical ignorance. It is a book that defeats itself and is an unfortunate addition to the legacy of an otherwise great scholar."

I wrote an email to Father Schall and informed him about Anderson's negative tweet. Father Schall, surprisingly, wrote:

"Thanks for these encouraging words from Anderson. I rather expected this would be the reaction from many. So be it."

I guessed that Father Schall cared less about Anderson's tweet and knew that many scholars would attack him for his critical position on Islam.

I continued to correspond with Father Schall via email as the Fall semester progressed. But our communication became less frequent because I was busy with new duties as a newly ordained deacon and being a full-time student at the same time. The fall semester ended and I had some time to rest and relax. Initially, I was planning to stay in Boston during Christmas because of my diaconate duty. Nevertheless, all the newly ordained Jesuits priests and deacons of the Jesuit West Province had to get together in Tucson, Arizona, from December 27 to December 30. I planned to visit California after my trip to Tucson.

While I was still recuperating from the fatigue of the Fall semester, I received the news that Father Schall was hospitalized; his intestines were wrapped around each other, causing a blockage that was potentially dangerous and quite painful. He was scheduled for surgery and had a small part of his intestine removed. I began to wonder whether Father Schall would be able to survive the surgery. Then the news came that although the operation was successful, the post-surgery recovery was an uphill battle for Father Schall. He was struggling because his digestive system had not begun to function properly, and he had to be re-admitted to the hospital.

At this point, it seemed the end was near for Father Schall, and I must find my way back to California to visit him. I was committed to serving as a deacon at Christmas Eve Mass in my parish, so I could not simply leave and go to California.

Nevertheless, I had a tiny window of time between December 25 to December 27 before the formation gathering in Tucson. Finally, I decided to change my plane ticket and fly to California on December 25 and fly to Tucson on December 27 in the afternoon. It cost me a lot of money to change the ticket, especially during the Christmas season, but this might be my last time to visit Father Schall.

On Christmas morning, I flew to California. I felt terrible for flying on Christmas when we are supposed to rest and reflect on the birth of Our Lord and Savior, Jesus Christ. Nevertheless, I found a little consolation in reading a book that I brought with me on the plane, *The Light of Christ: An Introduction to Catholicism*, by a Dominican Father, Thomas White, OP. Father Schall had long recommended I read this book; according to Father Schall, this book was more than an introduction. In Father Schall's view, this book was an excellent addition to classical literature on Catholicism, such as Joseph Ratzinger's *Introduction to Christianity* or G.K. Chesterton's *Orthodoxy*.

Father Schall was correct with his assessment; on my flight from Logan airport to San Jose airport, I found it delightful to read this book and I could not stop reading it. At every level, the book made me aware of the meaning and need for grace to reach an adequate understanding of what divine revelation reveals. In his book, White brilliantly explained how all elements of revelation are coherently interconnected and depend on each other. Revelation is often presented in the form of stories, myths, poetry, or analogy. But all these elements need clarification in the light of human beings' own experience and rational powers. We need to know that those stories, myths, or poetry are not contrary to reason. Here Catholicism has become the defender of reason, as it provides an intelligible explanation that what is revealed is defensible through reason.

Father Schall regularly spoke of the relation between Christian faith and human reason in terms of the relationship between political philosophy and Christian revelation. But how often do we hear about revelation during the Sunday sermon? Once, I had dinner with a priest who hold leadership position in the Catholic Church. This priest made a stunning confession that he never preached about revelation in his entire priestly career. It was a challenge for me as a future priest: how to preach about revelation in my future sermons.

My flight finally landed in San Jose airport, and I had almost finished the book. It turned out to be a meaningful Christmas day for me as I had a chance to reflect on the meaning of revelation on this Christmas day. It was already late at night when I arrived at Santa Clara Jesuit community. On the following morning, I called the Sacred Heart Jesuit Center and checked on Father Schall's whereabouts. The nurse told me that Father Schall had just returned home the day before.

I got to the Sacred Heart Center around 11 AM. Father Schall already had visitors when I arrived. He was sitting up in the lazy chair. The nurse reminded us not to overwhelm Father Schall and give him some space. Some ladies who seemed to already have spent a few hours or so with Father Schall graciously left the room and let me spend a little time with Father Schall.

"How do you feel, Father Schall?" I asked him.

"I can't see anything…. I feel helpless." For some reason, the surgery or the post-surgery recovery seemed to have affected his eyesight.

"Is there anything that I can do for you now?"

"Ask the nurse for my letters and read them to me." Many people sent Christmas cards, notes, or letters to Father Schall and his mailbox was piling up. I asked the nurse for Father Schall's letters and then read those letters to him. I recognize a few names, but most of them were from his friends, fans, or former students.

"Father Schall, this is a letter from the CUA press, and it seems that it contains a book contract for your book."[40]

"Oh, that's an important letter! Keep that document aside. I have to sign it."

I spent about half an hour reading him letters until his niece came in.

"This is my niece, why don't you introduce yourself?" said Father Schall to me.

I then introduced myself to Father Schall's niece, Collette, who came from Los Angeles to visit her uncle. I then observed Father Schall's interaction with his niece for a little while. After around 30

---

[40] The book was published posthumously by the Catholic University of American Press. Please see James V. Schall, S.J., *The Nature of Political Philosophy: And Other Studies and Commentaries.* (Washington, D.C.: The Catholic University of America Press, 2022).

minutes had passed, Father Schall seemed tired and said he might need to take some rest. Then he said:

"Why don't you take Collette for lunch upstairs? Find Ken Baker and introduce her to him."

"Okay, I will. But I want to let you know that I must go to Tucson tomorrow for a meeting for newly ordained Jesuits deacons and priests. So I might not be able to see you again after today."

In his thin voice, Father Schall said, "Just go. Thank you for visiting me. You are a good man and have much to give to the world, the Society, and the Church."

I did not know how to say goodbye, especially under the current circumstances and especially to a great priest like Father Schall. Finally, I just held his hand for a few seconds as my farewell.

"I think I'd better lie down now. Call the nurse to help me to go to bed."

I had lunch with Father Schall's niece, Collette, and we sat at the same table with Father Ken Baker as Father Schall instructed me to do so. During lunch, Collette shared her childhood memories about Father Schall, and Father Baker shared about his time with Father Schall in DC. One of his fond memories with Father Schall was on the inauguration day of Ronald Reagan in 1981, when they could not see anything because they stood so far away from the podium, except for Nancy Reagan's red dress. After lunch, we came back to the Infirmary and found that Father Schall was already taking a nap. In the meantime, more visitors and family members came to Los Gatos to see Father Schall. I finally decided to go back to Santa Clara.

On the following day, my flight to Tucson was supposed to leave in the early afternoon. But I decided to go back to Sacred Heart Center in the morning.

When I arrived, there were many visitors congregating in the Infirmary. The nurse said I must wait my turn because we must give some space to Father Schall. I waited for a little while, but there was no sign of the earlier visitors finishing their time with Father Schall. Then the nurse came with the news that she needed to clean the Father Schall's body, so all the visitors must leave the Infirmary. I was hoping to see Father Schall just one more time, but I didn't know whether I would have my last chance. In the meantime, daily Mass in the Sacred Heart Center was about to start. I decided to attend the Mass while waiting for my chance to visit Father Schall.

During the homily, I decided to sneak out of the chapel and see if there was a tiny chance for me to see Father Schall. The nurse finished washing him and said that I could come in. The other visitors seem to disappear, so this was the right time for me to visit.

"You are still here," said Father Schall.

"My flight is leaving in three hours, so I decided to visit you one more time. Do you feel stronger today?"

"No… I am still weak."

"Father Schall, there is something that I want to tell you. After our meeting yesterday, I have been thinking of writing a book about you, especially our friendship."

Father Schall nodded his head and said, "Good." I did not know what to expect, but it seemed that Father Schall gave his blessing for me to start this project.

"Thank you, Father Schall…. Oh yeah, I talked with Cindy yesterday about your situation, and she has been thinking of visiting you."

"If you talk with her again, send my love to her."

"I will."

"Rest seems to help the antibiotics that I am on. I want to go to bed now."

"Can I help you move to the bed?"

"No, you don't know how to do it. Find the nurse to help me."

I went out to find the nurse and told her that Father Schall needed help to go to bed. Before the nurse did her job, I held Father Schall's hand one more time and said that I was leaving now.

I don't know whether that was a proper way to say goodbye. But I finally had a chance to say goodbye to a great priest, scholar, friend, and father figure.

On the Death and Funeral

Miraculously, about a week after my visit, I heard from Cindy Searcy that Father Schall showed signs of recovery. Cindy finally flew to California and spent her time with Father Schall. According to Cindy, Father Schall was getting stronger daily and showed no signs of internal infection. I was busy with my comprehensive exam as part of the partial fulfillment for my Master of Divinity degree, so I did not have a chance to write to Father Schall immediately. On January 20, I finally emailed Father Schall to wish him a happy birthday and asked how he was doing. Father Schall wrote back to me and recommended that I read his latest interview with Kathryn Lopez about the question of life and death.[41] He also told me that he moved out of his regular room and was staying in a new room in the Infirmary.

February came, and we continued to correspond via email. On March 12, Father Schall wrote me an email:

"I hear that you are sentenced to St. Agnes in San Francisco for a year of visiting Bay area Indonesians, of whom there seem to be many. You could go back to Indonesia and be a martyr!"

---

[41] James V. Schall, S.J., "On Coming Back," Interview with Kathryn Jean Lopez, *National Review*, January 19, 2019, https://www.nationalreview.com/2019/01/father-james-schall-meditations-for-living/

I wrote back to Father Schall and thanked him for his note. I explained that after a lengthy discussion, the Provincial had missioned me to St. Agnes Parish in San Francisco, partially to work in the parish and partly to help the Indonesian Catholic community in the Bay area. The original plan of sending me to Alaska was falling apart because the Province consultors did not see the program as a good option. Finally, I told Father Schall that I did not need to go back to Indonesia to be a martyr because I might be persecuted and martyred even in San Francisco. Father Schall then wrote to me back that I might have my own "martyrdom" in St. Agnes. St. Agnes was a Jesuit parish that described itself as "an inclusive urban community, rich in diversity of age, ethnicity, gender, orientation, culture, talent, and treasure." I hoped that there was still space for a Jesuit like me at St. Agnes.

It turned out the email on March 12 was my last email exchange with Father Schall. Father Schall continued to send me his weekly articles or updates, until early April, but I did not have a chance to write back to him. His last email was dated April 5, in which he forwarded me an essay titled, *A Lesson for Pope Francis on Walls and Muslims.*

On April 8, I wrote him an email and tried to resume our old discussion about Notre Dame sports. Notre Dame Women's basketball team lost by 1 point to Baylor on the day before at the NCAA Championship final. I wrote to Father Schall that there were at least three exciting points from Notre Dame's loss to Baylor. First, Notre Dame was the defending champion: on April 1, 2018, with 0.1 seconds left on the clock, a guard, Arike Ogunbowale, hit a 3-pointer to give Notre Dame the NCAA championship over Mississippi State,

61-58. "It's Easter Sunday, and all the Catholics were praying for us," said Head Coach Muffet McGraw. A year later, Notre Dame tried to repeat the championship, but Coach McGraw, in her interview before the 2019 National Championship, said, "Faith did not us get here, Fighting Irish Spirit did." I am not sure whether she denied faith in Jesus Christ, but apparently, she did not think that prayers were needed any longer. In the end, the Fighting Irish Spirit did not help her team to win the championship.

Second, during the Final Four news conference, Coach McGraw gave a speech on women's equality and said she would not hire a male coach. Her statement was an echo of the statement from Notre Dame basketball star, Marina Mabrey, who tweeted that "to all the male, women's basketball haters, y'all can get in the kitchen and make us a sandwich now, thanks." Mabrey tweeted the message after Notre Dame won the NCAA championship in 2018.

I understood the frustration of those ladies because many men tend to look down upon women's sports, especially women's basketball. But I think that those ladies often forget that they still, to a lesser degree, owe their success to men. I imagine that many of them learned to play basketball from their fathers when they were young. At least they should give credit to their fathers or any father figures who taught them to play basketball in the first place.

Last, after Notre Dame lost to Baylor, all players and staff sat in a stone-quiet locker room where silence dominated. It was reported that out in the hallway, the University of Notre Dame President, Father John Jenkins, CSC, quietly walked past the locker room.[42] A year before, after Notre Dame won the championship, Father Jenkins stood outside the locker room, beaming while wearing a souvenir championship hat. In 2019, however, he said nothing to the losing team and barely looked up as he kept moving. I do not think Father Jenkins was doing the right thing as a father figure and priest. Father Jenkins knew how to dance during the victory, but he did not know how to act when the Lady Irish were beaten. I hoped Father Jenkins's action wouldn't generate more resentment from those young ladies. They might see the University President as a father figure, and what priest abandons their spiritual children when they are crushed.

I did not get a reply from Father Schall; I thought he considered my email a silly message and was not interested in women's basketball either. Nevertheless, I began to wonder what happened to Father Schall because even if my email was silly, he might still write back to me. Then I heard that Father Schall had been taken to the hospital and put in the ICU. No wonder that he never wrote back to my silly email! I continued to monitor Father Schall's health situation through his family's website, which was frequently updated by his nephew.

---

[42] Tom Noei, "Crushing conclusion to Notre Dame's national championship chase," *South Bend Tribune*, April 8, 2019. https://www.south-bendtribune.com/sports/college/notredame/a-crushing-conclusion-to-notre-dames-chase-for-a-repeat-national-championship/article_ccf898fe-8f4b-5e26-a104-b89d95c4fa3c.html

On April 15, a major fire erupted at the Notre Dame Cathedral in Paris. As fire devastated the Notre Dame Cathedral, people wept over the destruction of the building. But, I wonder, how many people cried because of the destruction of Western civilization that Notre Dame Cathedral represents? Fr. Schall was a vigorous supporter of Western civilization and, presumably, he would see the destruction of Notre Dame Cathedral as somehow symbolic of the destruction of that civilization.

Fr. Schall was a firm believer in Hilaire Belloc's famous remark that "Europe is the faith, and the faith is Europe."[43] Fr. Schall believed that this quote was correct because "Europe is where the Old Testament, New Testament, and Greek and Roman traditions melded with the so-called barbarians coming largely off of the Eurasian continent."[44] Of course, this fusion did not happen overnight; Europe as the bastion of Western civilization was built in the long span from the Fathers of the Church to the time of Aquinas. The construction of the Notre Dame Cathedral in Paris began in the 12th century when Europe's identity was solidified in the thought of many great Catholic thinkers. Thus, Notre Dame Cathedral was a symbol of Western civilization.

It is easy to rebuild the Notre Dame Cathedral as a building, but it is much more challenging to restore Europe's foundations. The French government, billionaires, and charitable groups can easily

---

[43] Hilaire Belloc. *Europe and the Faith*. (London: Constable & C., 1924)

[44] James V. Schall, S.J., "Belloc's Infamous Phrase," *The Catholic Thing*, October 18, 2011.

https://www.thecatholicthing.org/2011/10/18/bellocs-infamous-phrase/

donate money to restore the building of Notre Dame Cathedral. But those groups have far less interest in restoring the original vision of Europe. Two days after the burning of Notre Dame Cathedral, on April 17, 2019, Father Schall passed away. We can all mourn for the destruction of Notre Dame Cathedral and the death of Fr. Schall, but they both remind us that there is a more significant and challenging task ahead of us: to defend and rebuild Western civilization.

I could not describe my feelings upon hearing of the death of Father Schall. One of Father Schall's spiritual daughters, Jennifer Roback Morse, wrote something that rightly captured my feelings upon hearing of the passing of Father Schall. Ms. Morse wrote:

> The death of a father is an earth-shattering event. When my father died in 1993, I felt disoriented. I had never been to a world that did not include him. I could feel myself move up the generational ladder. No one is above me any longer. No one who matters stands above me… I thought of this when I learned that Father James V. Schall, S.J., had died. He was a father to me as to many. We have all just taken a step up the generational ladder. He won't be there anymore. Younger people will look to us now at times when we would have looked to him.[45]

---

[45] Jennifer Roback Morse, "On the Death of Great Men," *Crisis Magazine*, April 26, 2019. https://www.crisismagazine.com/2019/on-the-death-of-great-men

Indeed, Father Schall was not around anymore, and I had climbed up the generational ladder. In less than two months, I would be ordained as a priest, and many people would look to me now as a priest and a father figure as I used to look to Father Schall.

Father Schall's funeral took place on April 30, and I asked permission from my Rector at Boston College to attend the funeral in Santa Clara. I also requested permission from the acting Superior of the Sacred Heart Center that I might assist as a deacon at the funeral. Before the funeral mass, while I was vesting in the Sacristy, I met Father Joseph Fessio, S.J., who came to con-celebrate. I introduced myself to Father Fessio, and he asked me about my connection with Father Schall. I explained briefly to Father Fessio about our relationship, and then Father Fessio said, "You have to carry the legacy of Father Schall and continue to do his work." Of course, I felt that I had a responsibility to live up to the legacy that Fr. Schall left us. But I was also aware that no one could replace him, including me. At the very least, I could try to do something that Fr. Schall did for me: mentor and inspire numerous young people.

The funeral mass was quite simple and went well. After the funeral mass, while we were un-vesting in the Sacristy, Father Fessio said, "He is already meeting Augustine and Aquinas." Indeed, St. Augustine and St. Thomas Aquinas were the heroes of Father Schall, and they both were two heroes that represented his love for philosophy and theology. Like Father Fessio, I was sure that Father Schall would enjoy philosophical and theological discussions with St. Augustine and St. Thomas in the heavenly court.

We then moved to the Santa Clara Mission cemetery for the burial, where Father Schall's body was laid to rest at the old cemetery, alongside his Jesuit brothers. As his coffin was placed in the ground, I began to ponder that apart from meeting St. Augustine and St. Thomas Aquinas, Father Schall must also be looking forward to seeing St. Ignatius of Loyola in the heavenly court. St. Ignatius of Loyola, in his *Spiritual Exercises*, urges the person doing the exercises to choose a state in life—including what one's choices will look like "if I were at the point of death." St. Ignatius used this method because he knew how the Cross of Christ transforms the meaning of death. As a son of St. Ignatius of Loyola, Fr. Schall also knew that through his Cross, Christ had changed the definition of a good death into a good life. Moreover, Fr. Schall was ready to face death because he agreed with what his hero St. Thomas Aquinas said:

> *Christus autem satisfecit, non quidem pecuniam dando aut aliquid huiusmodi, sed dando id quod fuit maximum, seipsum, pro nobis. Et ideo passio Christi dicitur esse nostra redemptio* (now Christ made satisfaction, not by giving money or anything of the sort, but by bestowing what was of greatest price – Himself – for us. And therefore, Christ's Passion is called our redemption – ST. IIIa, Q. 48, c.).

In *paradisum deducant te Angeli*, Fr. Schall.

On Being a Priest of Jesus Christ

On June 8, 2019, I was ordained as a priest of Jesus Christ at Our Lady of Lavang Church in Portland, Oregon. Archbishop Alexander Sample ordained five Jesuits of the USA West Province of the Society of Jesus, including me. On the day before the ordination, we had lunch with Archbishop Sample. After lunch, I presented a little gift to the Archbishop, the book that I edited in honor of Father Robert Araujo, S.J., titled *Priests, Lawyers, and Scholars* with a foreword by Father Schall. As Archbishop Sample looked at the cover of the book, he immediately said, "Oh, a foreword by Father Schall. He was a great Jesuit priest." I was a little surprised but not shocked to hear that Archbishop Sample recognized Father Schall as a great Jesuit priest.

On the night before my ordination, I prayed and reflected on the language of Catholic tradition, which says that the priest speaks *in persona Christi*, "in the role of Jesus Christ." But the question is what kind of role must we play as a priest. My mind went back to a passage that Father Schall wrote in his book, *Catholicism and Intelligence*. Although I failed to review the book, I read the whole book and remembered a remarkable passage from it. Father Schall wrote that Christ "was not particularly concerned about this life but rather about our eternal life."[46] Father Schall argued that if we missed that end, we would miss the central point of Christianity. Father Schall wrote:

---

[46] James V. Schall, *Catholicism and Intelligence*, (Steubenville, Ohio: Emaus Road Publishing, 2017), 43.

Christ is a pious man. He does not dabble in or perfect literature, politics, art, technology, or science. As a carpenter, He produced no masterpiece that we can find in the British Museum. Even the often-eloquent words the evangelists attribute to Him are disputed by the Scripture scholars. What is left is the central point of Christianity. Christ dwelt among us essentially so that we would understand that eternal life is the reason for our creation.[47]

In the end Father Schall quoted Karl Rahner in his book on Spiritual Exercises that, "it is difficult for us to accept the fact that Jesus really cannot do anything else except save souls."[48]

What a remarkable passage! St. Ignatius of Loyola in the Principle and Foundation of the Spiritual Exercises said, "Man was created to praise, reverence, and serve God and, by these means, to save his soul." In his homily at his brother's funeral mass, Father Schall cited this passage and said, "these Ignatian points put things in their proper place. Whatever else we do, if we neglect this one responsibility, we miss everything."[49] Indeed, Father Schall was a truly a

[47] Ibid., 45.

[48] Karl Rahner, *Spiritual Exercises*, trans. Kenneth Baker, S.J. (South Bend, IN: St. Augustine Press, 2014), 123.

[49] James V. Schall, "May he now come in the presence of God Himself, the source of life and being," Sermon given at the Funeral Mass for Jerome Timothy Schall at St. Mark's Church in Boise, Idaho, on June 21, 2018. Catholic World Report June 24, 2018. https://www.catholicworldreport.com/2018/06/24/may-he-now-come-in-the-presence-of-god-himself-the-source-of-life-and-being/

modern son of St. Ignatius of Loyola. He understood that St. Ignatius wanted to help souls, and he composed Spiritual Exercises as a handbook for those engaged in helping souls to discern where God was calling them. Moreover, St. Ignatius realized that he could "help souls" better by becoming a priest. Later, St. Ignatius and his companions founded a new religious order, and they appropriated the name of Jesus because they wanted to follow Christ in saving souls.

Here I, about to be ordained as a priest of Jesus Christ, hoped that I could follow St. Ignatius of Loyola's path to walk with Christ to save the souls of many.

My Ordination Mass went smoothly, and it was the best day of my life. After the Mass, Archbishop Sample asked us to bless him, and I had the privilege to bless him first, and then he kissed my hands. As I walked back to the small chapel where the newly ordained priests vested, I felt that life was so beautiful. But something was missing; Father Schall was not at my ordination. I wished that Father Schall was there. I suddenly missed Father Schall, and then I know why. It was Saturday.

Afterword

I started working on this manuscript at the beginning of the Covid 19 pandemic and finished it in the summer of 2020. A lot has happened since I completed the manuscript. Firstly, Father Schall's prophecy came true when my pastoral year assignment at St. Agnes Parish in San Francisco proved to be a poor fit for me. Secondly, at the start of the pandemic, my biological father passed away in Indonesia. I didn't have the chance to go home for his funeral because the world was already closed. To be honest, I didn't experience my dad's passing as an earth-shattering event. I was shocked to receive the news, but I didn't feel disoriented since there had been a long distance between us. Nevertheless, his passing led me to reflect more on forgiveness. It's time for me to forgive my dad despite all his flaws and shortcomings. I should stop blaming everything on him and forgive all that he had done to me.

While the Covid pandemic was still affecting the world, I was given a new mission by my Provincial Superior that I had never imagined before in my life: to go to Rome and teach at the Gregorian University. I believe that Father Schall has interceded for me to receive this new assignment. I am also following in the footsteps of Father Schall, who used to teach at the *Instituto Sociale* at the Gregorian University in Rome from 1965 until 1977.[50] The *Instituto So-*

---

[50] Father Schall taught full-time at the Gregorian University's *Instituto Sociale* in Rome from 1965 until 1969. From 1969 until 1977, Father Schall taught the fall semester in Rome and the spring semester at the University of San Francisco.

ciale later became the Faculty of Social Sciences, and my new mission was to teach at the Faculty of Social Sciences at the Gregorian University.

I moved to Rome during the pandemic and started my new assignment at the Gregorian University. But, after living in Rome for two and a half years, my Provincial Superior summoned me to the final stage of Jesuit formation, known as tertianship. Jesuit formation is unique because it continues even after priestly ordination. Tertianship is usually a nine-month program involving spiritual training and apostolic ministry, occurring 3-5 years after ordination. During tertianship, a Jesuit revisits the founding documents and history of the Society of Jesus. Most importantly, during tertianship, a Jesuit once again makes the Spiritual Exercises of St. Ignatius of Loyola, spending 30 days in silent prayer, allowing the Holy Spirit to work in his life.

I left Rome in the late Spring of 2023 to start my tertianship. On the night before my departure, I remembered an essay titled "On Leaving Rome" written by Father Schall more than forty years ago.[51] I considered writing about my experience of leaving Rome, like Father Schall, and publishing it somewhere. But I decided against it because I'm not sure whether my departure will mark the closing chapter of my time in the Eternal City. During the tertianship, I should remain open to where the Holy Spirit will lead me, so there is always the possibility that I might return to Rome someday after my tertianship.

---

[51] James V. Schall, S.J., "On Leaving Rome," in James V. Schall, S.J., *Distinctiveness of Christianity,* (San Francisco: Ignatius Press, 1983).

Since finishing the manuscript and my time in Rome, I've been trying hard to find a publisher interested in my book. I reached out to about a dozen Catholic publishers, but unfortunately, none were interested; finally, on November 22, 2022, a Catholic publisher verbally committed to publishing the book in the Fall of 2023. But they kept delaying the contract. Then, on May 22, 2024, after waiting over a year, they suddenly said they couldn't honor their verbal commitment due to limited resources. This news was devastating, and I was on the verge of giving up on the project. I realized that if it's not God's will for this book to be published, I'm ready to let it go, just like Jesus's prayer in the Garden of Gethsemane: "thy will, not mine."

In the summer of 2024, despite feeling discouraged, some friends urged me not to give up hope. As a last-ditch effort, I sent a mass email to Father Schall's friends using his mailing list. I was overwhelmed by the response, receiving many suggestions from Father Schall's friends. Eventually, through a friend of Father Schall, I was connected with Mr. Sebastian Mahfood and En Route Books & Media. They showed immediate interest in publishing my manuscript and offered me a contract without hesitation. I am forever grateful to Mr. Sebastian Mahfood and En Route Books & Media for this opportunity.

Finally, I would like to express my gratitude to my Provincial Superior, Father Sean Carroll, S.J., for granting me permission to publish this book and Father Michael Gilson, S.J., the Socius of the Society of Jesus, USA West Province, for supporting this project. I am grateful to Father Paul Mariani, S.J., for his support and encouragement, as he is also trying to publish his book in a similar genre (I won the race by publishing this book earlier than him). I am also thankful to the Jesuit Community at Sacred Heart Jesuit Center in Los Gatos, California, where Father Schall spent the last six years of his life. Their warm welcome and hospitality during my frequent visits to Los Gatos to see Father Schall are deeply appreciated. In the spring of 2024, I spent some time at the Sacred Heart Center to take care on my health after experiencing some health concerns during my tertianship. I am grateful to the staff at the Sacred Heart Center for the care I received during my recovery. While at the Sacred Heart, I also had time to reflect on how much I miss Father Schall. This reflection reaffirmed my commitment to not give up on this project. As a friend of Father Schall once said we should pray that "Father Schall will never, not ever, be treated as a distant memory. It would be too grave a loss."[52] Lastly, as a member of the Society of Jesus, I want to thank Our Lord Jesus Christ for helping bring this project to fruition. Just as I pray like Jesus did in the Garden of Gethsemane, saying "thy will, not mine," I present this book with a prayer that God's will align with mine and that things work out to the greater glory of His name. *Ad Majorem Dei Gloriam.*

S. Hendrianto, S.J.
On the Feast of Our Lady of Rosary, 2024

---

[52] A private conversation with Maureen Mullarkey, August 24th, 2024.